This is Christianity

Book 1

Beginnings

Michael Keene

Stanley Thornes (Publishers) Ltd

First published in 1995 by:
Stanley Thornes (Publishers) Ltd
Ellenborough House
Wellington Street
CHELTENHAM GL50 1YW
England

96 97 98 99 00 / 10 9 8 7 6 5 4 3

A catalogue record for this book is available from the British Library.

ISBN 0–7487–1627–0

Printed and bound in Singapore by Craft Print Ltd

Acknowledgements

Ancient Art and Architecture Collection, p.5, 13, 60, 62; Andes Press Agency, p. 14 (right), 18 (left), 64, 71; ASAP, p.27, 30; Bridgeman Art Library, p.41 (*The Betrayal of Christ* by Giotto, c.1305 - Arena Chapel, Padua), 45 (*The Crucifixion* by Graham Sutherland - St. Matthew's Church, Northampton. © DACS, 1995), 51 (bottom) (*St. Peter* by Martino de Bartolommeo, 1369-1434 - York City Art Gallery), 56 (top) (*Emperor Constantine the Great*: Gold Aureus c.280-337 AD - Private Collection), 57 (*St. Peter baptising the Neophytes*. Detail from fresco by Masaccio c.1427, Brancacci Chapel, S. Maria del Carmine, Florence), 65 (top) (*Martin Luther's Sermon*, 1547, by Lucas Granach - Church of St. Marien, Wittenburg/Giraudon); Circa Photo Library, p.6, 12, 38 (right), 72; Frank Spooner Pictures, p.29, 34 (left); ICI Agrochemicals, p.31; Alexander Keene/Joanna Maclennan, p.11, 14, 18 (top and bottom right), 20, 21, 22, 24, 25, 36, 48, 74, 76, 77; Mansell Collection, p.65 (bottom), 66; Mary Evans Picture Library, p.63; Scala, p.56 (bottom); Sonia Halliday Photographs, p.8, 16-17, 43, 46, 53, 61; Spectrum Colour Library, p.59; Syndication International Ltd, p.34 (right); Trinity College Library, Dublin, p.58.

All other photographs supplied by the author.

Designed and typestyled by Janet McCallum

Illustrated by Gillian Hunt and Barking Dog Art

Throughout this book the terms BCE (Before Common Era) and CE (Common Era) are used instead of the more familiar BC and AD. However, in practice, they mean the same thing.

The bible extracts in this book are taken from the following:

Revised English Bible © Oxford University and Cambridge University Press 1989.

The Authorised Version of the Bible (The King James Bible), the rights in which are vested in the Crown, are reproduced by permission of the Crown's Patentee, Cambridge University Press.

Holy Bible, New International Version © 1973, 1978, 1984 by International Bible Society. Used by permission of Hodder & Stoughton Limited. All rights reserved.

Contents

Did Jesus really exist? – The evidence

Almost all of the information that we have about Jesus comes from the Bible. Before we look at this, we will look at the evidence for the existence of Jesus that we have from other sources. This does not amount to very much, but it does confirm that Jesus was a real person who lived, worked and died two thousand years ago in first-century **Palestine**.

Cornelius Tacitus (55–117 CE)

Tacitus, a Roman historian, explained how the Roman Emperor, Nero, (54–68 CE) had blamed the Christians in Rome for a fire which had burned down most of the city in 64 CE. As Tacitus pointed out, everyone knew that Nero himself had started the fire. Tacitus explained:

'Nero blamed and tortured a group of people hated for their evil practices – a group popularly known as Christians. Christ Jesus, from whom this group took their name, was put to death by Pontius Pilate, one of the Roman governors, during the reign of the Emperor Tiberius.'

Tranquilus Suetonius (69–140 CE)

Suetonius wrote about the Emperor Claudius, who had ruled the Roman Empire shortly after Jesus was crucified. He tells us:

'Christus [Christ] urged on the Jews, who kept causing a disturbance, so Claudius sent them away from Rome.'

There seems to be an error here. Can you see what it is?

The Talmud

Tacitus and Suetonius were both Romans. But we can also find information about Jesus in Jewish sources. The Talmud is a collection of Jewish writings put together from 70 CE onwards. All that it says about Jesus is that:

'On the eve of the Passover they hanged Jeshu [Jesus]. He practiced black magic and led Israel astray.'

How does this information from the Talmud fit in with what you know about Jesus from elsewhere?

Flavius Josephus (37–100 CE)

Josephus was a very important Jewish historian. He is our most important witness to the existence of Jesus:

'There was a wise man, Jesus, the son of Joseph. Many people thought he was a miracle worker. He taught people who wanted to learn the truth and he won over many Judeans [Jews] and many followers. Those who followed him thought that he was God's chosen leader. And when Pilate, at the suggestion of the principal men among us, had condemned him to the cross, those that loved him at the beginning did not forsake him; for he appeared to them alive at the third day, as the divine prophets had foretold.'

Timeline

Here is a timeline showing some of the people and events mentioned in this unit.

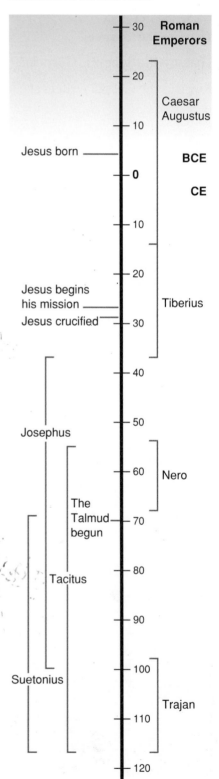

Josephus would seem to provide us with the most information about Jesus. However, there is a problem with it. Although Josephus was not a Christian, he seems to write like one, and this has made many people suspicious. They wonder whether later Christians tampered with his writings to make him seem more favourable to Jesus than he was. If this is the case, which words do you think are most likely to have been added? Why should anyone have done this?

- Where does most of our information about Jesus come from?
- Which Jewish book mentions Jesus?
- Which Jewish historian provides us with our most important evidence about Jesus apart from the Bible?

 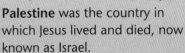

1

They really existed	They did not really exist	Not sure

Copy this chart into your book. Then write each of the names listed below in whichever column you think. Are you doubtful about any of them? Why are you so sure about most of them? Where has your information come from? If you are unsure, what kind of evidence do you need to be convinced?

Julius Caesar   **Henry VIII**   **William Tell**

St Nicholas   **Queen Elizabeth II**

Father Christmas   **Sherlock Holmes**

Oliver Twist   **Winston Churchill**

Robin Hood   **Jesus of Nazareth**

Is there a sense in which the characters from fiction 'exist' just as much as those from history? Think about it!

2 Divide a fresh page in your exercise book in the following way:

Cornelius Tacitus   **Tranquilus Suetonius**

The Talmud   **Flavius Josephus**

a Add brief notes to say what each of these sources tells us about Jesus.
b Bring all of these together to sum up, in a few sentences, what we know about Jesus from sources outside the Bible.
c Have you written down anything about Jesus that you believe to be untrue?

3 Here is a chance for you to do some of your own detective work. This is a famous 'picture' of Jesus. Can you find out:
a what this picture is imprinted on and what it is called?
b how this picture is thought to have been made?
c why so many people believe it to be a genuine imprint of the body of Jesus?
d why so many people doubt that this is a genuine image of Jesus?

4 Write the name of Jesus in the middle of the next clean page in your exercise book. Then, using the whole page, draw a chart like the one below.

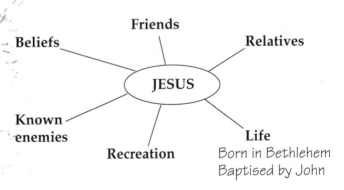

Fill in all that you know about Jesus on this chart. Some information has been given for you. Add more information to the chart as you discover more about Jesus.

What are the Gospels?

We have seen that we can only learn a little about Jesus from outside the Bible. Nearly all that we know about him is found in the four books at the beginning of the **New Testament**, known as the **Gospels**. The world 'Gospel' means 'good news', and was first used to sum up the actual teaching of Jesus. His message to the people was one of 'good news'. Before long, however, the word was applied only to those books in the New Testament which actually contained the story of Jesus' life and teaching.

Who wrote the Gospels?

We cannot tell just by reading the Gospels who wrote them or when. There is some evidence from the time to link the four books with four of Jesus' disciples, Matthew, Mark, Luke and John, and the Gospels are still called by their names today. Modern scholars, however, are doubtful about this, and think that, with the possible exception of Luke, the identity of the authors remains unknown.

You can discover what Irenaeus, an early leader of the Christian Church, had to say about the Gospel writers in Exercise 1. The problem is that he was writing in about 175 CE – over a century after the first Gospel was written. Does that make his evidence totally unreliable?

When were the Gospels written?

We cannot tell, either, just when the four Gospels were written. The original documents have long since been lost. There are one or two clues about when they were written, but most of it is guess-work. The small amount of evidence available would seem to suggest that:

- Mark's Gospel was written between 60 and 70 CE.

- Both Luke's and Matthew's Gospels were written around 80 CE, although we do not know which of them came first.

- John's Gospel was written around 90 CE.

Think about the implications of this for a moment. It means that the four Gospel accounts, upon which we depend so heavily for our information about Jesus, were written between 30 and 70 years after his death. Do you think that this presents a problem?

Scrolls from the Jewish Scriptures are still copied out by hand, as they were in the time of Jesus. Is it important to know who wrote the four Gospels?

For your dictionary

The **Gospels** in the New Testament were written by Matthew, Mark, Luke and John. They tell us about the life and teaching of Jesus.

The **New Testament** is that part of the Bible concerned with Jesus, whose coming was prophesised in the first part of the Bible – the Old Testament.

Why were the Gospels written so long after Jesus' death?

Jesus made a great impact on his followers, so why did they wait so long before writing a record of his life and teaching?

Reason One: In those days information was usually passed around by word of mouth. Little was put into writing. The first followers of Jesus kept his message alive by preaching to others about him.

Reason Two: As long as the disciples were still alive, the information about Jesus was safe. It was only when they became older and close to death that the need arose to write it down.

Reason Three: The early followers of Jesus thought that he would return to the world in their lifetime. It was only when they realised that this would not happen that they decided to set down a more permanent record.

It is possible that written records about Jesus existed before the Gospels. Indeed the Gospel writers may well have made use of them when they were writing their own accounts. However, if they did, no record of them remains. The four Gospels provide the only account we have of the life and teaching of Jesus of Nazareth.

- What is a Gospel?
- Which was the first Gospel to be written?
- How was the information about Jesus kept alive before it was written down?

1 Around 175 CE, Irenaeus, a Church leader, had this to say about the writers of the Gospels:

'Matthew published a written Gospel for the Jews in their own language while Peter and Paul were preaching the Gospel in Rome. After they died Mark, the disciple and interpreter of Peter, put into writing what Peter had preached. Luke, the follower of Paul, wrote down the Gospel Paul preached. Lastly John, the disciple of Jesus, set out the Gospel while living at Ephesus.'

a Irenaeus sets down clearly what he believed about the order in which the four Gospels were written. How does this order compare with what we now believe?

b In which language did Irenaeus believe the Gospel of Matthew had been written?

c From where did Mark obtain the information contained in his Gospel? How did he receive the information?

d Whose preaching forms the basis of Luke's Gospel?

e Where was John living when he wrote his Gospel?

2 Give a brief explanation of the following:

a Why we do not know who wrote the four Gospels?

b Why did the early Christians wait so long before writing down the story of Jesus?

c Is there any reason to think that one Gospel might be more accurate than the others? If so, which?

3 These are the symbols of the four Gospel writers – Matthew, Mark, Luke and John – known as the four Evangelists. Find out which symbol is which.

What are the Synoptic Gospels?

Where did Mark, the writer of the first Gospel, get his information about Jesus? He was not one of Jesus' original disciples, nor was he a leader of the early Christian Church. It is thought that Peter, the first leader of the Church, provided much of Mark's information. We do not know whether Luke and Matthew, writers of later Gospels, knew Mark's Gospel or copied freely from it. They would not have seen anything wrong in doing this, as copying from what other people had written was common practice.

This picture of Mark writing his Gospel comes from the Medieval period, one thousand years after the events of Jesus' life. At this time the invention of printing was still a long way in the future. How much work do you think was involved in painstakingly copying out a Gospel by hand?

Matthew, Mark and Luke

You may already have noticed that so far we have only been talking about three Gospels – Matthew, Mark and Luke – and yet there are four. Why has John's Gospel been left out? The reason is that this fourth Gospel is very different to the other three. Matthew, Mark and Luke often record events which John does not even mention. John writes about things that are not found in the other three Gospels. Because the Gospels of Matthew, Mark and Luke have so much in common, we call them **Synoptic Gospels**, from the Greek words *syn* ('together') and *opsis* ('view'). The fact that the three Synoptic Gospels have a similar approach to the life of Jesus is no coincidence. One of these three Gospels was probably written and circulated before the other two. The two later Gospel writers then copied freely from it.

There is another possible explanation. All three Synoptic writers could have copied from another account of the life of Jesus which has since been lost. However, it seems more likely that two writers copied from a third. If so, which was the first of the Synoptic Gospels to be written?

Which Gospel came first?

As we saw in the last chapter, Irenaeus thought Matthew's Gospel was the one from which the others took their information. Most people nowadays disagree with Irenaeus. They think that Mark's Gospel was used as the basis for the Gospels by both Matthew and Luke. Why are they so sure? There are three main reasons:

- Although Mark's Gospel is the shortest of the three, his version of events found in Matthew and Luke is longer than theirs. It seems more likely that Matthew and Luke condensed Mark's version of events when they wrote their Gospels.

- Almost all of the material recorded by Mark is found either in Matthew or Luke – or both. Out of the 661 verses in Mark's Gospel, an astonishing 631 are also to be found in the other two Gospels.

- Mark's account is a rough description of events compared to those found in Matthew and Luke. It is likely that they tidied up some of Mark's clumsier writing and improved on it.

The 'Synoptic Problem'

So, how did the Synoptic Gospels come into being? The chart below will help you to understand.

MARK

MATTHEW ← Q → **LUKE**

M

L

Do you notice something strange about this diagram? What do Q, M and L represent? Mark's Gospel was used as a source of information by the other two writers, yet both Matthew and Luke have material in common which does not appear in Mark. This means that they must have had access to another source of information – this is called 'Q' from the German word 'quelle' meaning 'source'. Matthew also has a little information not found in the other two Gospels (called M) and Luke likewise (called L).

- What are the Synoptic Gospels, and why are they called by this name?
- Which of the Gospels was the first to be written?
- What is 'Q'?

1 Look up and copy out each of the following short passages from the Gospels, setting them out side by side. Read each passage carefully.

- Matthew 8.1–4

- Mark 1.40–44

- Luke 5.12–14

a How can you tell that each of these accounts refer to the same event?
b Which close similarities can you find between the three accounts? Make a list of any words or phrases which occur in two, or three, of the accounts.
c Can you see any differences between the three accounts?
d Based on your observations, how convincing do you find the argument that Matthew and Luke copied Mark in writing their Gospels?

2 a Do you think it is possible for a writer to describe people or events without allowing his personal views to influence what he writes?

b All of the Gospel writers were committed followers of Jesus Christ. Does that mean that they were unable to write accurate and unbiased accounts of the life of Jesus? What do you think?

How did the Gospel writers see Jesus?

What do you think would happen if three of you were to write an account of the life of the same person who you all knew quite well? How similar do you think your accounts would be? Even if you do not agree on all the details, it is likely that your accounts would be equally 'truthful', but not necessarily identical. Each of you would have your own viewpoint about the person.

This was the situation with the writers of the three Synoptic Gospels. Each of them wanted to give a different picture of Jesus. Therefore, although they agree about Jesus' life as a whole, they disagree about the details.

Mark and Jesus

The events in Mark's Gospel move very quickly. He uses the word 'immediately' 41 times. Jesus is portrayed as a man in a hurry. Everything moves at a breathless pace, and before we know it we have arrived at the last few days in the life of Jesus.

In Mark's Gospel, Jesus is very much a human being, with all the weaknesses that human beings share. The sight of suffering moves him to pity; he shows anger; he loses his patience with his disciples; he is friends with a rich young man who is seeking eternal life, and he is afraid of his own forthcoming death.

Yet the same Jesus is more than human. He speaks with great authority; the winds and the waves obey him and he speaks openly of his approaching death.

Matthew and Jesus

Matthew wrote his account of the life of Jesus mainly for Jewish readers. In particular, he wanted them to know that Jesus was the promised **Messiah** of the Jews. For this reason Matthew frequently refers to the Jewish Scriptures to show that Jesus' life and death fulfilled all their prophecies about the Messiah.

As far as the Christians were concerned, Matthew was writing at a time when the newly-founded Christian Church was undergoing a severe persecution. He wanted to reassure the Church that its future was secure. He is the only Gospel writer to record the following words of Jesus to Peter:

'You are Peter, the rock, and on this rock I will build my Church.' (16.18)

Matthew also expected the world to end at any time. This was a belief held by all four Gospel writers, but Matthew placed a greater emphasis on it. He believed that when the world ended the Christian Church would not be destroyed.

Why did Matthew frequently refer to the Jewish Scriptures in his Gospel?

> **For your dictionary**
>
> The **Messiah** ('God's chosen one') was the leader the Jews were waiting for to deliver them from the oppression of the Romans.
> **Gentiles** was the name given to all non-Jews.

Why do you think it was unusual for a man to have sympathy for women in the time of Jesus?

Luke and Jesus

While Matthew wrote his Gospel for Jews, Luke was writing for non-Jews (**Gentiles**). He tells them that Jesus is for everyone, not just the Jews. He may have been the Messiah for whom the Jews were waiting but the Gospel – the 'good news' – that he came to offer was not only for the Jews. This comes out clearly in the parable of the Good Samaritan (Luke 10.25–37). The main point of the parable is that it was a Samaritan, from a tribe hated by all Jews, who stopped to help the man in trouble. In fact, in Luke's Gospel, Jesus constantly makes friends with those people who were the outcasts from society – the lepers, tax-collectors and others.

Luke also shows an understanding and sympathy for women, which was very much against the ways of society at this time! This sympathy is evident in the episode of the bringing back to life of the widow of Nain's son (Luke 7.11–17). In telling the story, Luke shows more sympathy for the feelings of the mother than the death of the son:

'*...the only son of his mother and she was a widow....*
When the Lord saw her his heart went out to her...'

- Who were the Jews waiting for to lead them out of Roman oppression?
- Who were the Gentiles?
- Which parable shows sympathy for a member of a race hated by all Jews?

1 Which Gospel...

a ...is the shortest of all?

b ...was written mainly for a Jewish audience?

c ...was mainly written for non-Jews?

d ...was written to show that Jesus cares for everyone, Jews and Gentiles?

e ...shows that Jesus shared many human weaknesses?

f ...shows that Jesus fulfilled many Old Testament prophecies?

g ...emphasises the sympathy of Jesus with all outsiders – including women?

2 a What is a biography?

b Do you think that the Synoptic Gospels are just three different accounts of the life of Jesus?

c Do you think that the three Synoptic Gospels could be put side by side to give us a 'complete' picture of the life and teaching of Jesus?

When and where was Jesus born?

Do you know in which year Jesus was born? Most people would think it was 0 CE. In fact, Jesus probably lived between 4 BCE and 29 CE. This may sound confusing. The reason is that a monk, centuries later, was four years out in his calculation of the year in which Jesus was born. We have lived with the consequences of his mistake ever since!

Palestine

Jesus was born, lived and died in Palestine, a small country no more than 270 kilometres long and just 80 kilometres wide at its narrowest point. The River Jordan divides the country into two halves, tumbling to over 400 metres below sea-level when it reaches the Dead Sea: the lowest point on earth.

Jesus was born in Bethlehem, but soon left this tiny village to grow up in Nazareth, in the district of Galilee. The people around him were deeply dissatisfied. They resented the fact that the Romans had occupied their country since 63 BCE, and there seemed to be no way for the Jews to regain their independence. The Roman stranglehold on Palestine was complete.

Jesus was a Jew

There has always been a simple way for deciding whether a person was a Jew or not – they must have a Jewish mother. Mary, the mother of Jesus, and Joseph, his father, were both Jewish. It was natural, therefore, for his parents to have Jesus **circumcised** when he was eight days old before presenting him in the **Temple** at Jerusalem a few days later (Luke 2.21). Jesus returned to the same Temple just after his twelfth birthday for his **barmitzvah** (Luke 2.41–52) and he took the opportunity to quiz the religious leaders there about faith in God. They were said to have been amazed at such understanding in one so young.

Later, when Jesus began to preach, he started in the **synagogue** where he worshipped regularly (Luke 4.16–30). At the end of his life Jesus went to Jerusalem with his disciples to celebrate the Jewish festival of **Pesach** (Luke 22.1–2). No doubt he celebrated the other Jewish festivals as well. Jesus was evidently very much a Jew. He was not a Christian. The first Christians did not appear until much later, after Jesus' death. It seems that Jesus never intended to start a new religion. He was born a Jew and died a Jew.

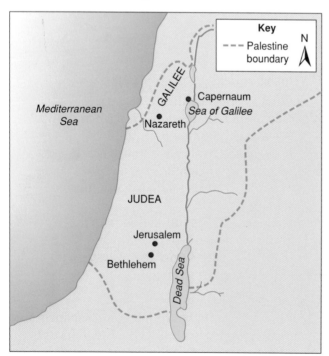

Which river bisected the country of Palestine and what was unusual about it?

Jewish boys today celebrate their barmitzvah on their thirteenth birthday. Was it the same in the time of Jesus?

The Romans

The Roman legions had marched into Galilee, Samaria and Judah back in 63 BCE and appointed **Herod the Great** as King of the Jews in 40 BCE. You can see how cruel Herod was by reading Matthew 2.16–18. Not surprisingly his death, in 4 BCE, was greeted with great relief by the Jews. His kingdom was then divided between his three sons.

The arrangement did not last long. Herod's son, Archelaus, was such a bad ruler that the Romans removed him and installed their own man (called a procurator) to rule Palestine. It was one such procurator, **Pontius Pilate**, who played a decisive part in the death of Jesus.

For centuries the Jews had been longing for the coming of a special leader, their Messiah, to deliver them from their enemies. For some time many of his followers wondered whether Jesus was this leader. It took them a long time to realise that the work Jesus had come to do was of a very different nature.

- When was Jesus probably born?
- Who was the Messiah and why did the Jews look forward to his coming?
- How was Jesus affected by his Jewish birth?

1 This is a picture of Augustus, who was Emperor of Rome between 14 BCE and 37 CE. Imagine you are Augustus. You want to make sure that Palestine, a small but important part of your Empire, remains peaceful and does not cause you any trouble. How would you set about it? Would you:

- make sure that someone from Rome who you trusted was put in charge of the country?

- dispatch as many soldiers as you could to Palestine to crush any signs of rebellion?

- appoint a Jew, who knew the people well, to run the country, whether he was liked by the people or not?

Well, what would you do? What did Augustus do? Did it work?

2 Make up some suitable clues to go with the answers in this word puzzle.

```
¹S
 Y          ²G
³N A Z A R E T H
 A          L
 G          I
 O          L            ⁵T
 G          E            E
 U    ⁴J E R U S A L E M
 E                       P
                         L
                         E
```

How was Jesus baptised and tempted?

Who was John the Baptist? What part did he play in the early story of Jesus? Why did Jesus come to him in the desert to be baptised? What happened after Jesus was baptised? Who was the Devil? As we begin to study the life of Jesus, we will be looking for answers to these questions.

John in the Gospels

John the Baptist played an important part in the story of Jesus, yet he only makes a brief appearance in the Gospels. He:

- preached to the people and baptised them;
- baptised Jesus;
- was imprisoned and met his death at the hands of King Herod.

But that is all!

John and his work

John the Baptist, a wild and noisy character, seems to have come out of the desert wearing a rough coat of camel hair. He was a cousin of Jesus and appears to have survived on a diet of locusts and wild honey! Today such a figure would make headline news, but at that time people were familiar with people like John. They had been brought up on stories of the great **prophets** of the past, like Moses and Elijah. John was simply another prophet – sent by God to prepare the people for the coming of Jesus.

He told the people that they needed to change their lives before they could follow God. This change, called repentance, could only take place in the heart. **Baptism** is an outward sign for everyone to see that an internal change has taken place. The people flocked to John to be baptised in the murky waters of the Jordan as a sign that this inner cleansing had taken place.

Along with many other people, Jesus joined John's movement. He came forward to be baptised. John was taken by surprise. He wondered why Jesus, who was sinless, should come along to confess his sins like everyone else. Can you think of any reason why Jesus should have wanted to be baptised by John? Compare your answers with Matthew 3.14–15.

We are told that when Jesus came up out of the water after being baptised by John, he, but no one else, heard the voice of God and saw the Holy Spirit of God come down to him like a dove. It probably did not happen quite like that. In fact, we cannot be sure of just what took place. What we do know, however, is that Jesus regarded this event as the beginning of his public work.

Do you know of any churches in which you might see events like these taking place? Only one of these events closely resembles John's method of baptism. Which is it?

The temptation of Jesus

Nor can we be sure what happened shortly afterwards. We do know that Jesus spent six weeks **fasting** in a desert area like the one shown in the picture.

At the end of this time, we are told, Jesus was tempted by the Devil, **Satan**, in three ways. You can read about these temptations for yourself in Matthew 4.1–11. By reading carefully you will also discover how Jesus overcame each of the temptations.

In the time of Jesus most people believed in the Devil as the source of evil, as many people still do today. The majority of people now believe that their doubts and temptations come from within themselves, not from without. Perhaps the temptations of Jesus make more sense if we think of them in this way. What do you think?

- What did John the Baptist try to tell the people?
- Why was John surprised when Jesus came to be baptised?
- How did Jesus deal with each of the temptations?

Why does this desert area seem a suitable place for the temptation of Jesus?

1 Mark's description of the temptations of Jesus is very brief:

'*At once the Spirit drove him out into the wilderness, and there he remained for forty days tempted by Satan. He was among the wild beasts; and angels attended to his needs.*' (Mark 1.12–13)

a What is another name for 'Satan'?
b Who drove Jesus out into the wilderness?
c Who tempted Jesus whilst he was in the wilderness?
d Why do you think that the temptations of Jesus are said to have taken place in the wilderness?

For your dictionary

Baptism is the ceremony by which people are initiated into the Christian faith.
Fasting is when a person goes without food, usually for a religious purpose.
A **Prophet** is a man or woman who passes on God's message to the people.
Satan, the 'Accuser', was the leader of the evil spirits opposed to God in Jewish and Christian belief.

'Repent and believe'
says desert preacher

2 This headline might have appeared in the *Nazareth Echo* at the time of John the Baptist.

Write a newspaper account in no more than 200 words that might have appeared under this headline.
Remember – all newspaper accounts are short, snappy and to the point.

15

Who were the friends of Jesus?

Was Jesus a loner? Did he travel around Palestine on his own teaching, preaching and healing? No. One of the first things he did was to choose a band of close friends to accompany him. However, there must have been many times when he regretted having to share his life with others. Do you ever feel like that?

The Disciples

A Jewish teacher (**rabbi**) always collected his own circle of **disciples**. Jesus was a rabbi and had his own band of followers. Amongst them were:

- his chosen twelve disciples (the Apostles), who were all men;

- 70 followers who were sent out by Jesus to preach and teach;

- a group of women who were committed followers, including his own mother and Mary Magdalene;

- many ordinary people who travelled from place to place listening to him.

Jesus spent most of his time with twelve Jewish men whom he chose personally – his disciples. He shared his whole life with them. You can find out how they were chosen by reading Luke 6.12–16. Of this group, Peter, James and John were the closest to Jesus – a kind of inner circle – especially towards the end of his life. You can find out how these three disciples came to leave their full-time occupation of fishing to share a simple life with Jesus by reading Luke 5.1–11.

Bartholomew (Nathaniel) died as a martyr.

James, the son of Alphaeus, was put to death by being sawn in half.

Andrew, the brother of Simon Peter, was crucified upside down on an X–shaped cross.

Judas Iscariot was treasurer for the disciples. He betrayed Jesus for a reward of 30 pieces of silver, but later regretted it and committed suicide by hanging himself.

Misunderstandings and desertion

Although Jesus spent much of his time teaching his disciples, they did not always understand what he was trying to say to them. On one occasion, for example, Jesus warned his disciples that he was shortly to be put to death in Jerusalem, and Peter tried to dissuade him. The disciple was rebuked sharply by Jesus:

'Out of my sight, Satan….You think as men think, not as God thinks…'

In fact, all of his disciples deserted Jesus when he needed them most – as his death approached. To save his own skin Peter even denied knowing Jesus. The women followers acted more courageously. Mary Magdalene, another Mary and Salome were amongst a group that watched from a distance as Jesus was put to death.

Simon Peter, whose name was Simon but Jesus called him Peter ('the rock'). He was a fisherman, denied Jesus before the Crucifixion, became the most important leader in the Early Church, and was himself crucified upside down in Rome.

- What is a disciple?
- Which disciple became the leader of the early Church?
- Which disciple betrayed Jesus?

James, older brother of John, was a fisherman. He was one of the 'inner circle' of disciples, and was finally martyred by being beheaded.

Matthew (Levi) was a tax-collector.

Judas (Thaddaeus) became a missionary.

Simon, the Zealot, probably belonged to the **Zealot** political party before becoming a disciple.

Thomas (Didymus) expressed doubts after the resurrection of Jesus, and was martyred as a missionary in India.

John, brother of James, was called, along with his brother, the 'sons of thunder' because of their fiery temperament. The Gospels tell us that he was 'the disciple that Jesus loved most'.

Philip was called to follow Jesus along with his friend Nathaniel.

Read Mark 14.66–72 carefully before answering the following questions:

a   What was Peter doing in the courtyard of the High Priest?

b   Who was the first person to challenge him?

c   How did the bystanders pick Peter out?

d   What do you think this incident tells us about friendship?

e   Put yourself in Peter's shoes and explain how you felt after you had denied Jesus.

(You can look up Luke 22.60–61 to find out what actually happened to Peter after his denial of Jesus).

2   The names of eleven of the twelve disciples are hidden in this wordsquare. Can you find them?

A	Z	P	J	I	E	W	O	U	O	P	B
X	T	H	O	M	A	S	U	N	M	S	A
L	V	I	U	F	N	V	H	R	W	Y	R
T	U	L	A	G	D	W	D	P	J	Q	T
N	A	I	K	Q	R	G	P	Q	U	T	H
O	L	P	E	T	E	R	F	V	D	L	O
E	R	H	A	Z	W	M	L	R	A	C	L
J	O	H	N	B	X	M	T	C	S	D	O
A	S	I	J	K	K	X	S	E	R	N	M
M	U	I	J	L	S	I	M	O	N	Z	E
E	V	T	H	A	D	D	A	E	U	S	W
S	G	H	M	M	A	T	T	H	E	W	B

Which of the disciples is missing?

Jesus – a worker of miracles?

It was the Jewish historian, Josephus, you may remember, who described Jesus as a 'wonder-worker', and the Gospels tell us that Jesus performed many **miracles**. But what kind of happening are we really talking about? What kind of 'wonder-worker' was Jesus? How did he regard his own miraculous powers? What kinds of miracles did he perform?

Do you think that any of these are miracles?

The miracles of Jesus

According to the Gospels, Jesus performed three different kinds of miracle:

He fed the hungry

One story in the Gospels, above all others, illustrates the belief of the early Christians that Jesus had extraordinary power over the ordinary things of nature. This particular story was thought to be so important that we have it in the Gospels, in some form or other, no less than six times!

Do you remember the story of Jesus feeding a large crowd of people with just five loaves of bread and two small fish? Look up the story in Matthew 14.15–21.

Why is this such an important miracle? To answer this question you must know a little background information. The ancestors of the hungry people in front of Jesus had also been fed miraculously by God as they wandered in the desert centuries earlier. Where was Jesus feeding the people? In the desert! The same power had been shown by God and by Jesus! Jesus must have been someone special – the Jew's Messiah.

He healed the sick

As one of his first acts in public, Jesus went into a synagogue on the **Sabbath Day** (Luke 4.16–21). He read a passage from the Jewish Scriptures which declared that God's chosen messenger, the Messiah, would make:

- the blind see,
- the deaf hear,
- the lame walk,

and this is just what Jesus did. To the Gospel writers this was the clearest possible proof that Jesus was God's Messiah.

He had power over nature

In the four Gospels we read that Jesus:

- calmed a storm at sea;
- turned water into wine at a wedding;
- walked on water and frightened his disciples;
- instructed his disciples where to make an overwhelming catch of fish;
- told his disciples where to find money to pay their taxes in the mouth of a fish;
- destroyed a fig tree when it did not bear any fruit, even though it was out of season.

What do you think about these miracles? Why do you think that many people find these the most difficult to believe of all Jesus' miracles? Do you find some more believable than others?

How did Jesus see his miraculous powers?

We know that there were many 'miracle-workers' around at the time of Jesus who did not waste any opportunity to show off their 'miraculous' powers. However, Jesus seems to have been very different to them. He used his powers only very sparingly, and made every effort to keep them secret – although many of those he healed could not keep the secret quiet for very long! Jesus looked upon his miracles as 'signs' that he was someone special, but he refused to use his powers to put on a 'miracle show' just to please, or impress, others.

- What is a miracle?
- What different kinds of miracle is Jesus believed to have performed?
- Which of Jesus' miracles are more difficult to believe in than others?

1 Read John 6.1–13. Imagine that you are a reporter who is present at this event. Prepare a script for a television programme to explain to viewers what you saw.

Remember – you need to include both what you saw Jesus doing *and* the reaction of the crowd.

2 Read Luke 17.11–19 before answering the questions.

As Jesus was travelling towards Jerusalem he passed through Samaria and Galilee. As he was entering a village he met a group of lepers. Leprosy was believed to be a disease that could be passed on very easily. People who suffered from leprosy were often forced to live apart from other people.

a What did the lepers call out to Jesus?
b What did Jesus tell them to do?
c What happened next?
d Copy the following paragraph into your book, filling in the blanks as you write.
'_____ of them, finding himself _____ , turned back with shouts of '_____ to God'. He threw himself down at _____ feet and _____ him. And he was a _____ . At this _____ said: "Were not all _____ made _____ ? The other _____ , where are they? Was no-one found returning to give _____ to _____ except this _____ ?" And he said to the man, "_____ up and go on your way; your _____ has made you _____ "'
e What do you think Jesus meant when he said that the leper's faith had made him whole?

How did Jesus teach the people?

Jesus taught his disciples and all the people who followed him a great deal about God, life and himself. Sometimes he spoke simply, in short sentences, so that people could more easily remember what he had taught them. Often he used stories, or **parables**, to make it easier for people to understand and remember his message. How many of his stories can you remember?

The parables

Jesus was not the only storyteller of his time. Many people moved around the countryside telling their stories to anyone who would listen – young and old. However, Jesus does seem to have been very good at telling stories. This was important, as most of his followers were uneducated people, and telling them stories was the best way of getting his message across clearly.

The stories that Jesus told are very special. He wanted to teach through his stories and that is why they are called 'parables'. A parable is a story which carries a particular meaning or message, although not everyone manages to understand it! On one occasion Jesus even suggested that he told his stories to make the truth *more* difficult to understand! His parables were both word-pictures and puzzles which needed to be thought about carefully in order to understand their message.

Why do you think that Jesus did not simply spell his message out in words of one syllable?

What makes a good teacher?

What was 'God's kingdom'?

Some of the stories told by Jesus may seem rather strange to us today because he used images and ideas that were familiar to his listeners 2000 years ago. Some of the familiar experiences which Jesus used in his stories were:

- a farmer sowing seed.

- a lost sheep.

- a woman sweeping her house to find a lost coin.

- people looking after a vineyard.

Most of the stories that Jesus told were about 'God's kingdom'. This phrase would have made sense to his listeners. Every Jew looked back a thousand years in their history to the time when King David ruled over Israel. Since that 'Golden Age' they longed for the coming of a second David. So when they heard Jesus speak about God's kingdom, they thought this was what he meant. In fact, when he used this phrase, Jesus was speaking of the 'kingdom' which is created every time God comes to rule in a person's heart and they start to love and serve one another. You will find out more about this important part of the message of Jesus in the chapter called 'What was God's kingdom?'.

The Good Samaritan

A lawyer once asked Jesus the question 'Who is my neighbour?'. Jesus replied by telling him the parable illustrated in the stained glass window shown here, and recounted in Luke 10.29–37 – The Good Samaritan. You probably know it very well, but it always helps to find out something about the background to a parable. In this case we can understand the message of the parable more clearly if we know that:

- the road from Jerusalem to Jericho was wild and desolate with only the occasional inn to offer refreshment to the weary traveller. Brutal robberies took place every day on this road.

- using a Samaritan as the hero of the story would surprise, and shock, Jesus' Jewish listeners. The Jews and the Samaritans had been sworn enemies for centuries.

Why, then, did Jesus choose a Samaritan as the central character? Jesus wanted to force his listeners to face up to their own prejudices. By telling this story, Jesus not only answered the lawyer's question but went much further to teach his listeners an unforgettable lesson. That is true of many of his parables.

- What is unusual about a parable?
- What are most of the parables of Jesus concerned with?
- What parable did Jesus tell to answer the lawyer's question 'Who is my neighbour?'

For your dictionary

A **parable** is a story drawn from nature or from everyday experience to teach a particular religious or moral message.

Can you work out which well-known parable of Jesus is illustrated in this stained glass window?

1 Jesus did not always use parables to teach. The Beatitudes are a collection of his most famous sayings. You can read them for yourself in Matthew 5.1–11. When you have read them carefully, match up the correct halves of each beatitude and copy them into your exercise book.

	Blessed are...	They will...
a	the poor in spirit:	be comforted.
b	those who mourn:	inherit the earth.
c	those who hunger and thirst for righteousness:	be shown mercy.
d	the merciful:	have the kingdom of heaven.
e	the pure in heart:	be called the sons of God.
f	those who are persecuted:	see God.
g	the meek:	they will be filled.
h	the peacemakers:	have the kingdom of God.

3 Make up your own parable based upon this young child. Make the parable as relevant as you can to life today. Remember – a parable must be a good story which makes a clear religious or moral point.

2 Someone said that listening to a good story is rather like peeling an onion. What do you think they meant?

What did Jesus teach about forgiveness?

Forgiveness was one of the main themes in the teaching of Jesus. First, and most important, was the possibility of us being forgiven by God. Jesus taught that God is always waiting and ready to forgive. The problem lies in our willingness, or unwillingness, to forgive each other.

Lost and found

As we have seen, Jesus often taught in parables. Three of his most popular parables, which you can read one after the other in Luke 15, have a common theme:

- The lost sheep.
- The lost coin.
- The lost son.

The theme is that of being lost, being found and being welcomed home again. In the case of the lost son, the most important of the three parables, the welcome given to the son when he returns home is the main point of the parable.

This photograph shows Christians celebrating the service of Holy Communion. Try and think of the different ways in which we can sin against God and other human beings, as in the Act of Penitence.

Repent and be forgiven

Do you remember John the Baptist? He preached to the people that they should repent of their sins and ask God for forgiveness. They should then be baptised as a sign that they had repented. You may remember that part of the Lord's Prayer is a request for God's forgiveness although, to be forgiven, a person must first forgive others.

Prayers of penitence (being sorry for what you have done wrong) have always played a central part in Christian worship. This is particularly true in the service celebrating **Holy Communion** where the Act of Penitence is very important.

The Act of Penitence in the Anglican Church goes like this:

Almighty God, our Heavenly Father,
we have sinned against you and against our fellow man,
in thought and word and deed,
through negligence, through weakness,
through our own deliberate fault.
For the sake of your Son, Jesus Christ,
who died for us,
forgive us…

The Lost Son

Of the three stories that Jesus told about forgiveness, the best-known is that of the Lost Son. With so many children and young people running away from home each year (about 10,000 in England alone) the story seems very relevant to our own time.

In the story that Jesus told there are three main characters – a father and two sons. The youngest son takes his third of his father's inheritance and squanders it until he is left with nothing. He is finally forced to take a job feeding pigs, a job which, for complicated religious reasons, no self-respecting Jew would dream of doing. He returns very reluctantly to his father, hoping to be taken on as a servant, and finds that his father is waiting to welcome him home again as his son.

If the father in the story represents God and the lost son the sinner, as they appear to do, what do you think Jesus was trying to teach us through this parable? What about the complicating factor of the elder son who is not happy to see his brother come home? Who, do you think, does he represent?

- Which three parables of Jesus all have the common theme of forgiveness?
- What, according to Jesus, is necessary before forgiveness can take place?
- What is the main lesson to be learned from the parable of the Lost Son?

1 This is what Jesus said about forgiveness in the Lord's Prayer:

'Forgive us the wrong we have done,
As we have forgiven those who have wronged us.'

a Does this suggest that God does not forgive us unless we are prepared to forgive other people?
b If so, do you think that this is fair?

2 The parable of the Lost Son can be looked at through the eyes of three people – the father, the younger son and the elder son. Draw up a chart in your exercise book like the one below and then summarise what we learn about each character from reading the parable.

The character	What we know about them
The father	
The younger son	
The elder son	

3

FOURTEEN YEAR-OLD GIRL LEAVES HOME AFTER ROW WITH FATHER

Fifteen year-old boy runs away from home after crashing father's car

Boy runs away after setting fire to parents' home

a Each of these headlines has a sad story behind it. Take one of them and write a brief account of what that story might be.
b Take one of these stories and describe briefly what you think might be going through the mind of a mother or father as they wait for some news about their son or daughter.
c Do you think that if each of the runaways went home their parents would forgive them? Would you?

Did Jesus believe in prayer?

What do you think prayer is? Some people describe it as 'speaking to God'. Speaking to God was as natural to Jesus as talking with his disciples. It was something that he usually chose to do when he was alone – often at times when he faced a crisis in his life or had an important decision to make. The Gospels tell us of many times when Jesus went off by himself to pray. He also taught his disciples how to make prayer an important part of their own lives.

The Shema

Growing up in the Jewish faith, Jesus would have been taught to pray at an early age. He would have recited the most important Jewish prayer of all – the Shema – each morning and evening. This prayer was a direct quotation from the Old Testament book of Deuteronomy and it is still said daily by Jewish people today:

Hear, O Israel, the Lord your God is one Lord, and you shall love the Lord your God with all your heart, and with all your soul and with all your strength.
(Deuteronomy 6.4–5)

What do you think praying might mean to this child?

Jesus' parables about prayer

Jesus taught that one of the most important things in the family of God is to be able to talk to the Father. He bitterly attacked those who made it difficult for others to pray. His own prayers, as you will see in Exercise 1, were simple and direct. He addressed God as *Abba* ('Daddy'), in contrast to most Jews of the time, who used the equivalent of the more formal 'Father'.

Jesus told several parables to teach people how to pray. In particular, he wanted to teach his followers that 'they should always pray and never be discouraged' (Luke 18.1). You can read one such parable for yourself in Luke 11.5–8, although you need to know two facts before the story can have its full impact:

- At the time of Jesus, long journeys in Palestine were normally taken at night to avoid the intense heat of the day.

- It would have been unthinkable to refuse hospitality to a traveller no matter how inconvenient it might be.

In Jesus' parable, a traveller arrives unexpectedly at a friend's house at midnight. The host is unprepared, and goes to a neighbour's house to ask for food for the visitor. The neighbour at first refuses to get up and give him anything, but the parable tells us that, in response to the host's continued knocking, the neighbour will give him what he asks.

What do you think this parable was intended to teach us about prayer? If you think of the obvious, it is probably right!

Jesus summed up his teaching about prayer in three words: Ask, Seek, Knock.

God is far more willing than a human parent to respond to the requests of his children. Does that mean that God always answers our prayers? That is not an easy question. What do you think?

- What is the Shema?
- Which three words sum up Jesus' teaching about prayer?
- What word did Jesus use to talk to God when he prayed, and what did it mean?

1 Copy this table into your exercise book.

Bible reference	Why did Jesus pray?

Look up each of the following references and list on the table the occasions when Jesus is said to have prayed. In each case, give a reason why Jesus was praying.

- Mark 1.35; 6.41; 8.6.
- Mark 14.35–36.
- Mark 15.34.
- Luke 6.12–13.
- Luke 10.21–22.
- Luke 11.1.
- Luke 23.34; 23.46; 24.30.

2 You can find a story that Jesus told about prayer in Luke 18.2–8. Read it carefully.

a Make up a modern story which makes the same point as this story told by Jesus.
or
b Tell the story in the form of a poem.
or
c Explain in your own words what lesson about prayer you think Jesus was trying to teach in this parable.

3 These comments about prayer were made by three young people.

a Read them carefully, and explain in your own words what you think they are saying.
b Do you agree with them or not? Give your reasons.
c When do you think that prayer might help someone?

John, age 14

'I pray sometimes. I should pray more often, but I usually pray when I'm in some kind of trouble. I'm not sure whether it really works, but it seems to help.'

Anne, age 15

'I try to pray every day. Praying to God is rather like speaking to my parents. The lines of communication break down from time to time, as they do in every family, but it is not long before they are restored.'

Alan, age 13

'I find that praying does work. God does not always answer in the way that I expect – or hope! Sometimes the 'answer' is totally different to what I expect. I have learned to accept that. After all, God knows a lot more than I do!'

Who opposed Jesus?

Jesus made many friends but he also made some influential enemies. The Gospels make it clear that most of the considerable opposition to Jesus came from the two most powerful religious groups of the time, the **Pharisees** and the **Sadducees**.

At times Jesus was openly very critical of both groups, and said some unflattering things about them! They in turn thought that Jesus was betraying his Jewish background and leading the people astray. There were probably misunderstandings on both sides. Why were these two religious groups at loggerheads with Jesus? To answer this question we must take a closer look at the two groups involved.

What complaint would Jesus have had against a Pharisee (right) and a Sadducee (left)?

The Pharisees

Members of this Jewish group were wealthy merchants who believed that they could best serve God by keeping themselves and their religion 'pure', by avoiding all contact with non-Jews (Gentiles). The Temple in **Jerusalem** was a beautiful building with several courtyards. The closer a person got to the centre of the Temple, called 'The

Holy of Holies', the holier they became. The Temple authorities (mainly Pharisees) believed that Gentiles would 'contaminate' the holy places and so confined them to the outer courtyard.

Jesus did not agree with this. Not only did he believe that the Temple, as God's House, should be open to all, but he ate with the very people that the Jewish leaders despised. He even suggested that these very 'sinners' might enter heaven before the Jews themselves – a remark hardly likely to make him popular with the Jewish religious leaders! Why do you think he said it?

The Sadducees

This influential group was made up of wealthy people in the city of Jerusalem. Many of them held powerful positions in the **Sanhedrin** – the Jewish Council which met in Jerusalem to solve religious problems, gather taxes and serve as a law court. The Sadducees were unpopular with other Jews because they supported the Romans.

Read the Gospels and you soon become aware of the one issue that separated Jesus from most of the religious leaders – what could and could not be done on the Sabbath Day.

For your dictionary

Jerusalem was the capital city of Palestine, founded by King David.

The **Pharisees** were a powerful religious group in the time of Jesus and their name means 'the separated ones'.

The **Sadducees** were an influential religious group who supported the Romans.

The **Sanhedrin** was the highest Jewish court. It had 71 members and met in Jereusalem.

- What was the Sanhedrin?
- What were all Jews forbidden to do on the Sabbath Day?
- Which two religious groups, according to the Gospels, gave most opposition to Jesus?

The Sabbath Day

Most of the disagreements that Jesus had with the religious leaders in Jerusalem were over the keeping of the Sabbath Day. This was a very important issue for Jews, then as now. The word 'sabbath' means 'to break off' and refers to the day on which all work stopped. It is the holy day set aside for the worship of God and the study of the Scriptures. It runs from sunset on Friday through to sunset on Saturday of each week. According to the Gospels, there were many times when Jesus was accused of breaking the Sabbath laws. You can look up the following for yourself:

1 Matthew 12.1–8 Jesus allows his disciples to pick corn and eat it.

2 Matthew 12.9–14 Jesus heals a man with a withered arm.

3 John 5.1–15 Jesus heals a crippled man.

Why do the Gospels present Jesus and the religious leaders as being in opposition from the very beginning? Could it be that some of the later hostility between Jews and Christians was written back into the story of Jesus?

This is part of a model of the Temple as it would have been at the time of Jesus. It shows the holiest part of the Temple. What was this called?

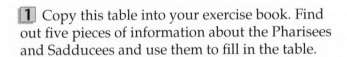 1 Copy this table into your exercise book. Find out five pieces of information about the Pharisees and Sadducees and use them to fill in the table.

	The Pharisees	The Sadducees
1		
2		
3		
4		
5		

a In what ways do you think the two groups were similar?

b In what ways were they different?

2 Read carefully this passage from Matthew 9.10–12:

'When Jesus was having a meal in the house, many tax-collectors and sinners were seated with him and his disciples. Noticing this, the Pharisees said to his disciples, "Why is it that your teacher eats with tax-collectors and sinners?" Hearing this he said, "It is not the healthy who need a doctor, but the sick."'

Why do you think Jesus said this to the Pharisees?

3 This is what the Jewish historian, Josephus, had to say about the beliefs of the Sadducees:

'They believe that man has a free choice of good and evil, and that it rests with each man's will whether he follows the one or the other. As for the survival of the soul after death, punishments in the underworld and rewards, they will have none of them.'

Put into your own words two beliefs held by the Sadducees.

'Who do the people say that I am?'

There is often a turning-point in a person's life when something very important happens to them. Perhaps you know of someone who has just experienced such a turning-point? For Jesus, his watershed happened at Caesarea Philippi, a small town about 40 kilometres north of the Lake of Galilee. This town was the capital of the territory ruled over by Herod Philip, one of the sons of King Herod the Great.

Why were the events at Caesarea Philippi so important in the life of Jesus?

Who was Jesus?

Who was Jesus of Nazareth? Everyone had been talking about it and, not surprisingly, the disciples had discussed it amongst themselves. Was Jesus really the Messiah that all Jews had been longing for – or not? If he was, why did he not just say so and admit it? If not, then who was he? With all the talk that was going on, the mystery surrounding Jesus simply deepened. No wonder the disciples were mystified.

When Jesus arrived at Caesarea Philippi with his disciples, he asked them a leading question: *'Who do the people say that I am?'*

They replied, *'Some think that you are Elijah; others that you are John the Baptist brought back to life and still others that you are a prophet.'*

Then Jesus asked them the most direct question of all: *'What's your opinion? Who do you think I am?'*

It was Simon, so often the spokesman for the disciples, who spoke up. He said, *'You are the Messiah.'*

This was a momentous declaration. It was the first time that any of the disciples had publicly expressed what they thought about Jesus. It was an important turning point in the life of Jesus, and nothing was ever quite the same afterwards.

Peter – the rock

Jesus was overjoyed at Simon's statement. He said that Simon was not simply repeating what other people were saying. God alone could have revealed this truth to him. At the same time Jesus gave Simon a new name – Peter ('the rock'). You can read about all this for yourself in Matthew 16.13–20.

What was the significance of Peter's change of name? Christians have never agreed about this. There are two possible interpretations:

1 Roman Catholics believe that Peter himself was the rock (foundation) upon which the Christian Church was built. As the first Bishop of Rome, Peter was succeeded by other Bishops, or **Popes**. Each of them inherited the power and authority first given to Peter by Jesus.

2 Protestants do not believe that Peter became the first Bishop of Rome or that the Pope is the head of all Christian Churches. They believe that when Jesus said 'on this rock I will build my church' he was referring to Peter's declaration of faith and not Peter himself.

1 Here are four comments about Jesus which came from a class of 12 year-olds.

Anne

'A very special man. God's Son. Yes, very definitely, God's Son.'

Julian

'Someone sent by God to tell us how we should live. Pity he ended up being killed for what he said.'

Sue

'Sometimes I think there was something remarkable about Jesus but other times I am not so sure.'

Andrew

'There have been many unusual people in history. Some of them have founded religions. Jesus was no different. He was one of these people.'

Now try to sum up what *you* believe about Jesus.

For your dictionary

The **Pope** is the head of the Roman Catholic Church with his headquarters in the Vatican, in Rome.
Protestants belong to Christian Churches which have broken away from the Roman Catholic Churches.
Roman Catholics belong to the Church which accepts the authority of the Pope.

- What had the people been saying about Jesus when he arrived at Caesarea Philippi with his disciples?
- Who publicly acknowledged Jesus as God's Messiah at Caesarea Philippi?
- What name did Jesus give to Peter after his declaration, and what did it mean?

2 Find out the following facts.

a How many Popes have there been since Simon Peter?

b Why did the Bishop of Rome become known as the 'Pope'?

c What is the name of the present Pope and which country does he come from?

d What do Roman Catholics believe to be the link between the present Pope and Simon Peter?

3 This is the symbol of St Peter – an upside-down cross and two keys.

a Can you find out why an upside-down cross is associated with Simon Peter?

b Read Matthew 16.19 and then write a short explanation of why two keys are part of St Peter's symbol?

What happened at the Transfiguration?

Simon Peter was the first person to call Jesus the Messiah, the Son of God. From that moment onwards, Jesus began speaking openly about the suffering and death that lay ahead of him. He also said that he would rise from the dead after three days.

What was the Transfiguration?

Shortly after the events at Caesarea Philippi Jesus climbed with his three closest disciples – Peter, James and John – to the summit of a mountain. He wanted to spend some time quietly praying with them. We do not know which mountain they climbed. For a long time it was thought to be Mount Tabor, but that is little more than a hill. It is much more likely to have been Mount Hermon, which was close to Caesarea Philippi and much higher than Mount Tabor.

The location is not as important as the event which took place when the four of them reached the top of the mountain. Jesus was transfigured – his appearance changed completely – and both the prophets **Moses** and **Elijah** appeared to him. Mark describes in his Gospel what happened next:

'In their presence he was transfigured; his clothes became dazzling white, with a whiteness no bleacher on earth could equal.' (Mark 9.2–3)

Why should Moses and Elijah have appeared to Jesus? There are two important reasons:

- Both Moses and Elijah had also had an experience of God on a mountain.

- To the Jews, Moses was the great giver of the Law (it was to Moses that God had given the Ten Commandments), whilst Elijah was the greatest of the prophets.

Tabernacles

It seems that the extraordinary events of the Transfiguration took place at around the Jewish festival of **Sukkoth** (Tabernacles). At this time of the year Jewish people made shelters or tabernacles out of greenery. As you can see from the photograph, this festival is still celebrated in the same way today. Jewish people live in these shelters for a few days to remind themselves of their ancestors who lived in tents for 40 years after they left slavery in Egypt.

When Peter saw Jesus talking with Moses and Elijah he suggested that they should build shelters like these for the three of them. At that moment a cloud covered them all (symbolising the presence of God) and a voice was heard to say: *'This is my beloved Son: listen to him.'* (Mark 9.7)

Can you remember another occasion, at the start of Jesus' ministry, when a voice was heard from heaven? What was the occasion? What did the voice say?

For your dictionary

Elijah was the most important of the Jewish prophets, who lived in the ninth century BCE.
Moses was the Jewish leader and prophet who led the Israelites out of slavery in Egypt.
Sukkoth is the Jewish festival of Tabernacles.

These Jewish people are celebrating the festival of Sukkoth or Tabernacles. How is this festival celebrated?

The descent from the mountain

On the way down from the mountain, Jesus told the three disciples to say nothing about what they had seen until after he had risen from the dead. They did not understand what Jesus was talking about and they asked why the prophets had said that Elijah must come back before the Messiah could die and rise from the dead. Jesus explained to them that Elijah had already come back and had been treated very badly. He was referring to John the Baptist. However, the disciples still failed to understand what Jesus was trying to tell them.

- Who went with Jesus up to the summit of the mountain, and why?
- Who appeared to Jesus and his disciples on the mountain?
- What did the voice from heaven say?

Mountain tops were considered the most likely locations for people to hear the voice of God. Have you ever climbed a mountain? If so, can you explain why mountains have so often been associated with experiences of God?

1 Read the following accounts of how Moses, Elijah and Jesus experienced the voice of God. Then answer the questions about each account.

a Read **Exodus 19.17–25**.
What happened when God came down to the mountain? What was the reaction of the people? Who was the only person allowed to meet with God?

b Read **1 Kings 19.8–12**.
What happened to Elijah on the mountain? Where did he find God?

c Read **Mark 9.2–13**.
Who appeared to Jesus and the disciples on the mountain? What effect did this have on the disciples?

d Imagine that you are a witness to one of these events. Write a short account of what you have seen and the effect it had on you.

2 According to the Old Testament, Moses had a similar experience to that of the three disciples. This is how it is described:

'Moses went up Mount Sinai and a cloud covered it. The dazzling light of the Lord's presence came down on the mountain.' (Exodus 24.15–16)

Can you find three close similarities between the experience of Moses and that of the disciples during the Transfiguration of Jesus?

3 You can find out what happened when Jesus came down from the mountain after he was transfigured by reading Mark 9.14–27.

What were the Scribes and Pharisees arguing about? Either in your own words or with drawings, show how the story ends.

What was God's kingdom?

Imagine that you are a Jew living in Palestine at the time of Jesus. Six centuries earlier your ancestors had fought a war against the Babylonian invaders – and lost. The Babylonians were followed by the Persians and then the Greeks, who had kept up the pressure on your people. After a short spell of freedom, the Romans came and took over your country. The last thing you want is to be ruled by foreigners. You wanted God to be in charge of your country, and no-one else.

God's kingdom in Palestine

To want God to be your ruler was a good idea in theory. What, though, did it mean in practice? There were plenty of ideas on the subject at the time:

- The **Essenes** believed that God would destroy all evil in his kingdom.

- The Zealots wanted to launch a war against the Romans under the leadership of God's Messiah. Their message was to banish the Romans and set up God's kingdom.

- The Sadducees had come to terms with the Romans. They caused the Romans no trouble. The Romans recognised them as the leaders of the Jewish community.

What did Jesus teach about God's kingdom?

Jesus often spoke of the Kingdom of God. However, he did not mean quite the same thing as many other Jews when they used the term. Jews taught about the Kingdom of God in parables. Here are just two of them:

Mark 4.26–29 The Kingdom of God is like seed which a man scatters on the ground. Whether the man constantly watches it or not the seed grows – night and day. The man does not know how it happens. By itself the seed produces corn – first the stalk, then the ear and then the full grain – which is then harvested.

Mark 4.30–34 The Kingdom of God is like mustard seed – the smallest seed that can be sown. Once in the ground it becomes the largest of plants. In fact, its branches are so large that birds are able to come and make their nests in its branches.

'Love one another'

The Gospels make one thing very clear about God's kingdom: anyone can belong to it. You do not have to be a Jew, a religious person or even particularly good. When you join you become part of God's community. In that community there are very few rules. In fact there is only one, and Jesus summed this up when he told his disciples:

'I give you a new commandment: love one another; as I have loved you, so you are to love one another.' (John 13.34)

Jesus often used this image of corn and harvesting in his parables to teach about the Kingdom of God. How did he use it in Mark 4.1–20, and what does this tell us about God's kingdom?

For your dictionary
The **Essenes** were a strict sect that lived apart from other Jews.

Jesus said that this love has to be directed in two ways:

- Towards God – those in God's kingdom must love God with all their heart, soul, mind and strength.

- Towards each other – after loving God the most important commandment in God's kingdom is that everyone should love their neighbour – as they love themselves.

Some Jews thought of God's kingdom as a political kingdom. To Jesus this kingdom was more concerned with the heart and relationships.

- What did the Jews mean by 'the Kingdom of God'?
- What did Jesus mean by this?
- What did Jesus say that everyone must do in order to belong to God's kingdom?

1 We have seen how Jesus used the image of corn and harvesting in his parables.

a Read Matthew 13.24–30.

b What do you think Jesus was telling his listeners about God's kingdom in this parable?

c Now read Matthew 13.36–43, in which Jesus explains the parable. How near were you?

2 You have read that Jesus used familiar images from everyday life and nature in Palestine to teach people what the Kingdom of God was like.

Supposing that Jesus was teaching today, make up two modern parables to illustrate truths about God's kingdom. Make sure that your parables use aspects of life with which we are familiar today.

3 A lawyer once approached Jesus and asked him which of the Ten Commandments were the most important. Jesus replied that all ten could be summed up in just two:

'The most important one is this: Hear, O Israel, the Lord our God, the Lord is One. Love the Lord your God with all your heart, and with all your soul, and with all your mind and with all your strength. The second is this: Love your neighbour as yourself. There is no commandment as great as these. (Mark 12.29–31)

Re-write Jesus' answer in your own words.

Was Jesus on the side of the outsiders?

An 'outsider' is someone who for some reason does not really 'fit' into their group, class, family or community. They do not conform to the accepted rules of that group or society. There have been outsiders in every age and place. You can probably think of groups of people who fit this description today. Jesus met many people who simply did not seem to fit in.

Zacchaeus

According to Josephus, the Jewish historian, Jericho was a place where 'the palm trees grew and that balsam which is the ointment of all the most precious.' Jericho was also the home of one of the most unlikely of all the followers of Jesus – Zacchaeus. This man was a tax-collector, employed but despised by the Romans and hated by all of his fellow-Jews. He was very wealthy, but he had accumulated his wealth by illegal means, so he had few friends. He also had another problem – he was very small, and that gave him an inferiority complex. He was so small, in fact, that he had to climb a

sycamore tree to see Jesus when he visited Jericho. When Jesus passed down the road he saw Zacchaeus perched in a tree over the road and invited him to come down.

'Zacchaeus, be quick and come down, for I must stay at your house today.' (Luke 19.5)

For a rabbi to speak to an 'outsider' like Zacchaeus was considered highly unusual, but for a rabbi to visit the home of a tax-collector was just not done. Jesus' disciples let him know what they thought. For Zacchaeus the event changed his life. After meeting Jesus he promised to pay back four times the amount that he had overcharged anyone and give half of his possessions away to the poor.

In return Jesus promised both Zacchaeus and his family that they were 'saved'. What do you think he meant by this?

Zacchaeus showed by his actions that he was willing to change his life. Perhaps you know of someone whose life has changed direction? Certainly the attitude of Zacchaeus is very different to that of a rich young ruler who came to question Jesus.

Which of these photographs shows people who would be considered by our society as 'outsiders'?

The rich young ruler

This man appeared to have everything he could want, yet he came to Jesus to find out what he had to do to gain eternal life. Jesus reminded him of the commandments from the Jewish Scriptures:

- Do not commit adultery.
- Do not murder.
- Do not steal.
- Do not give false evidence in court.
- Honour your father and mother.

Without hesitation, the man said that he had kept all of these commandments since he was a child. He was a very good Jew. Jesus saw the problem and put it directly to the young man:

'There is one thing you lack. Sell everything you have and give to the poor, and you will have treasure in heaven; then come and follow me.' (Luke 18.22)

This came as a great surprise, both to the man and to everyone listening. Luke tells us that the man's heart 'sank' – he was very upset. His Jewish faith had taught him that wealth was a sign of God's blessing. But Jesus was suggesting that wealth can be a barrier to anyone wanting to enter God's kingdom. He used the familiar sight of a camel to underline what he was saying:

'It is easier for a camel to go through the eye of a needle than for a rich man to enter the Kingdom of God.' (Luke 18.25)

Why do you think that everyone was so amazed at what Jesus said?

- Why were tax-collectors some of the most hated members of the Jewish community?
- What was unusual about Jesus speaking to Zacchaeus and visiting his house?
- What did Jesus say would prevent the rich man from entering God's kingdom?

1 Read Luke 19.1–10.

a Where did Zacchaeus live and how is he described?

b What did he need to do when Jesus visited his city, and why?

c Why did the people disapprove of Jesus eating with Zacchaeus?

d What job did Zacchaeus do?

e What did Zacchaeus do to prove that he was willing to change his lifestyle?

2 a Can you think of three groups in our society who are frequently viewed as 'outsiders'? Can you explain why in each case?

b Do you think that most of us treat outsiders well – or not? Can you think of any ways in which our treatment of them could be improved?

3 Read Matthew 19.16–24, his account of the meeting between Jesus and the rich young ruler.

a Which commandments did Jesus suggest that the ruler should keep?

b What was the ruler's response?

c Does Jesus seem to have accepted the ruler's answer?

d What did Jesus say in reply?

e What can we learn from this encounter about the attitude of Jesus towards wealth and money?

What happened in the last week?

If you have been to a carnival or fair recently you can probably imagine what the streets of Jerusalem were like each year at the festival of Pesach (Passover). They were crowded with jostling people and animals, noisy and very excited. We know that Jesus had visited Jerusalem before for this festival – can you remember when?

Jesus arrives in Jerusalem

The last week in the life of Jesus began as he made his way to Jerusalem, with his disciples, for the Pesach celebrations. Everyone looked forward to celebrating the time, centuries earlier, when their ancestors had escaped from slavery in Egypt. For this festival, which was held in April, Jews travelled to the capital city of Jerusalem from all parts of the Roman Empire. Most of them walked to the city, but Jesus arrived in a very unusual way – on a donkey. Christians today often re-enact the entry of Jesus into Jerusalem on **Palm Sunday**.

Matthew tells us that the whole city went wild with excitement. The people laid their coats on the road and ripped down palm branches. What was Jesus trying to do? Was he trying to force a showdown with the political and religious leaders? Certainly the Jews and the Romans must have been very worried about the excitement he was causing.

The explanation was very simple. Jesus was fulfilling a prophecy made centuries earlier in the Jewish Scriptures by Zechariah:

'Tell the city of Zion (Jerusalem), look, your king is coming to you! He is humble and rides on a donkey.' (Matthew 21.5)

Do not forget that the Jews would have known this quotation well. They would have understood quite clearly what Jesus was claiming to be – a king!

The last week of Jesus' life

Following the dramatic entrance of Jesus into Jerusalem, events moved very quickly towards his death on the cross.

Monday   Jesus violently overturns the desks of the money-changers and traders working in the Temple.

Tuesday   Jesus teaches the people in the Temple and is questioned by the Pharisees, the Herodians and the Sadducees. They try to catch him out – but fail.

Wednesday   Judas Iscariot makes an offer to the Chief Priest – he will betray Jesus for 30 pieces of silver.

Thursday   Jesus and his disciples eat their last meal together in an upper room in Jerusalem. Afterwards they go to the **Garden of Gethsemane**, where Jesus is betrayed and arrested.

Friday   Jesus is tried by:

— **Caiaphas**, the High Priest.

— Pontius Pilate, at the Governor's residence.

— Herod, in the fortress of Antonia.

Jesus is executed at **Golgotha**.

What are the people in this procession celebrating?

- What is the name of the day on which Christians celebrate the entry of Jesus into Jerusalem on a donkey?
- Which Jewish festival was being celebrated when Jesus entered Jerusalem?
- How was Jesus received by the people of Jerusalem?

For your dictionary

Caiaphas, the Jewish High Priest at the time of the arrest of Jesus, was the son-in-law of the previous High Priest, Annas.

The **Garden of Gethsemane**, close to the Mount of Olives, was the place where Jesus was arrested.

Golgotha was the place where Jesus was crucified.

Palm Sunday marks the beginning of Holy Week.

1 a Read Matthew 21.8–11, and then copy out the following paragraph, filling in the blanks as you go.

A large crowd of people spread their _____ on the road whilst others cut _____ from the trees and spread them on the road. The crowds walking in front of _____ and those behind began to shout, 'Praise to _____ _____! _____ bless him who comes in the _____ of the _____! _____ _____!

When _____ entered _____, the whole city was thrown into an _____. 'Who is he?' the _____ asked. 'This is the _____ _____, from _____ in _____', the crowds answered.

b Imagine that you had been one of the crowd in Jerusalem on this occasion. Write a short letter to a friend describing the excitement that you had witnessed.

2 *'Blessed is he who comes in the name of the Lord.'*
a Who said these words?
b What was the occasion?
c What did the people think when they saw Jesus riding on a donkey?
d What was Jesus actually saying by his actions?

3 Copy this map of the city of Jerusalem as it was in the time of Jesus. How many places can you see which are mentioned in the text on this spread?

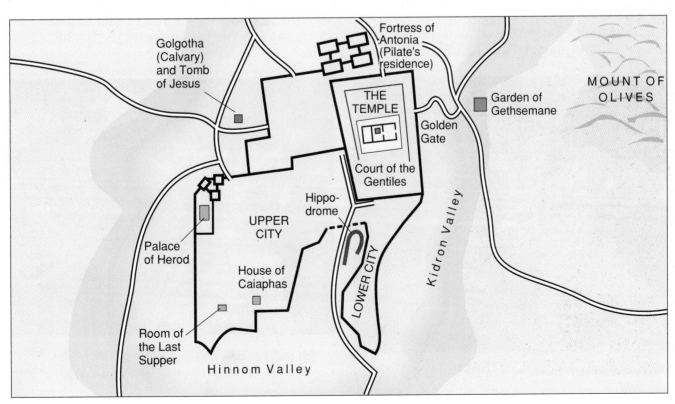

What happened at the Last Supper?

At the centre of the Jewish festival of the Passover there is a special meal called the Seder meal. All the members of the family come to the meal, at which special food is eaten to remind everyone of the journey of the Israelites out of slavery in Egypt.

Jesus celebrates the Passover

Jesus made arrangements to eat the Seder meal with his disciples. They ate it together in the upstairs room of a house belonging to a friend in Jerusalem. While they were celebrating the Pesach together, Jesus told his disciples some disturbing things which they did not fully understand until much later.

Jesus told the disciples that one of them was going to betray him into the hands of his enemies. Can you imagine what effect this revelation must have had on the disciples as they sat around the table? They were even more disturbed when Jesus told them that they would all desert him when he needed them most. Peter protested and said that he would follow Jesus anywhere – even if it meant he had to die by doing so. These words were soon to sound very hollow indeed!

Jesus then took a piece of bread, thanked God, broke it and distributed it amongst the disciples.

He had often done this before. But this time, as he handed each of them a piece of bread, he said:

'This is my body which is given for you. Do this in memory of me.' (Luke 22.19)

The Seder meal always ends with everyone sharing a glass of wine together – the 'cup of blessing'. On this occasion, as Jesus passed the cup around, he said:

'This is my blood which is poured out for many; my blood which seals God's covenant.' (Mark 14.24)

The bread and the wine

Jesus was giving the bread and wine to his disciples as symbols of his body, which was going to be broken (the bread), and of his blood, which was going to be spilt (the wine) when he died only a few hours later. Whenever his followers came together in the future, they would share bread and wine with each other and remember the death of Jesus on the cross.

Most Christians today try to put these words of Jesus into practice. Nearly all Churches have a special service at which they eat bread and drink wine together. The exceptions are the **Quakers** and the **Salvation Army**. Depending on which Church you belong to, the service will be called either Holy Communion, the Eucharist, the Divine Liturgy, the Mass or the Lord's Supper.

What event in Jewish history is celebrated at the Passover?

Which two symbols are used in the service of Holy Communion to remind worshippers of the death of Jesus?

Jesus washes the disciples' feet

After the disciples had eaten together they began to argue amongst themselves over which of them was the most important. What they were concerned about was which one of them would become the leader after Jesus had died. To settle their quarrel, Jesus acted out a parable in front of them. Wrapping a towel around his waist and taking a bowl of water he began to wash their feet. This was a task normally carried out by the lowest servant in the household. What do you think that Jesus was trying to teach his disciples?

For your dictionary

The **Quakers** began in around the year 1650 through the teachings of George Fox.
The **Salvation Army** is a branch of the Christian Church which started in the last century.

- Which Jewish festival did Jesus celebrate in the upper room with his disciples?
- What did Jesus tell his disciples that disturbed them so much?
- What lessons did Jesus teach his disciples using the symbols of bread, wine and water?

1 At a modern Seder meal the youngest member of the family asks the question 'Why is this night different from all others?' On the table in front of the family are pieces of 'matza' (bread without yeast) and a dish which contains, amongst other things, a lamb-bone and bitter herbs. The drinking of wine is a very important part of the meal.

Can you find out the symbolic importance of:

- the matza.
- the lamb-bone.
- the bitter herbs.
- the wine?

'When I eat the bread and drink the wine I feel very close to Jesus, and that is very important to me. Holy Communion helps me to put my life into perspective.'

2 At the Last Supper Jesus told Peter:

'I tell you before the cock crows twice tonight you will deny me three times.'

a Find out when these words of Jesus came true.
b Can you imagine why Peter, and the other disciples, should desert Jesus at the very time when he most needed them?

'I really don't understand Holy Communion. All I know is that it helps me as a Christian to think back to the death of Jesus and to try to follow his teachings more closely.'

3 Tom and Sue are two young Christians who regularly attend Holy Communion at their local church. This is how they describe the importance of the service to them personally.

How do these two comments help you to understand what Holy Communion means to Christians today?

How was Jesus betrayed and arrested?

After the Last Supper, events leading to Jesus' death the following morning happened very quickly. When Jesus left the upper room with his disciples, he crossed over the valley of the River Kidron and came to a garden of olive trees called Gethsemane, which stood on the lower slopes of the Mount of Olives. It was here, in the next few hours, that Jesus spent what were probably the most difficult moments of his life.

The Garden of Gethsemane

Jesus took Peter, James and John (his closest disciples) with him into the remotest parts of the Garden of Gethsemane. His mood was very sad and serious. He felt that all the powers of evil were organised against him. His friends, though, did not understand the agony he was suffering. What do you think was disturbing Jesus so much?

To help him come to terms with what was going to happen to him, Jesus went on further by himself and began to pray. He was very much afraid of what was to come. Although he knew there was no other way to save God's people and to avoid the suffering, he still prayed:

'Father! All things are possible to you. Take this cup of suffering from me. Yet not what I want but what you want.' (Luke 22.42)

From this photograph, what do you think Jesus did in the Garden of Gethsemane?

Three times Jesus returned to his disciples, only to find them sleeping each time. When he returned the third time, he suddenly knew what God wanted him to do, and accepted it. He told his disciples:

'Look! The hour has come. Look, the Son of Man is now being handed over to the power of sinful men.' (Matthew 26.45)

Just as he said this, Judas arrived with a group of soldiers, and a few moments later he was arrested.

The betrayal and arrest of Jesus

Those who came to arrest Jesus were members of the Temple Guard, probably supported by a few Roman soldiers. Judas approached Jesus and kissed him. It was a sign of courtesy and respect to greet a teacher (or rabbi) with a kiss. However, in this case the kiss was a symbol of betrayal. It was a pre-arranged sign between Judas and the soldiers to identify Jesus. You can almost imagine the tears in the eyes of Jesus as he asked:

'Judas, would you betray the Son of Man with a kiss?'

At that moment something extraordinary happened. Most travelling Palestinians at this time carried a heavy knife or a short sword for protection against wild animals or bandits. Jesus' disciple, Peter, drew his sword and slashed at the head of the Chief Priest's servant, Malchus, and cut off his ear. Jesus did not need that kind of protection. He touched the man's ear and it was healed.

At that moment the disciples ran into the darkness. One of them was almost caught, but wriggled out of his tunic and ran off leaving it in a soldier's hands. The soldiers thought about going after him but they were only really interested in arresting Jesus. They were content now that they had their prisoner. They led Jesus away to the headquarters of the High Priest.

- Where did Jesus go after his last meal with his disciples?
- What did Jesus hope to avoid when he prayed to God?
- Who betrayed Jesus and how did he do it?

This is a medieval painting of the arrest of Jesus. Why is a kiss a particularly sad form of betrayal?

1 We are not told why Judas betrayed Jesus. This seems rather odd. Why do you think we are not told? Do you think it was because:

- the reason did not matter. The only important thing was that Jesus had been betrayed?

- the Gospel writers knew the reason, but they did not want anyone to know that a disciple of Jesus could have betrayed him for such a reason?

- the writers believed that God had planned it so that Judas betrayed Jesus?

- no one knew the reason, since no one knew what was going on inside Judas' head?

a Which of these do you think is the **most** likely explanation, and why?
b Which of these do you think is the **least** likely explanation, and why?

c Can you think of any other possible explanation?
d From what you know about Jesus, what do you think might have happened if he had met Judas after the betrayal?

2 The photograph of the Garden of Gethsemane may help you to imagine the scene when Jesus was arrested. Certainly the time that he spent there, his betrayal by Judas and his arrest by the guards are amongst the most dramatic moments in the whole of the Bible.

In groups of about eight, act out the scene of the arrest of Jesus. Afterwards, write down briefly how you think each of the following might have felt as events unfolded:

a Jesus.
b The disciples.
c Judas.
d The soldiers.

How was Jesus tried and condemned?

According to the Gospels, Jesus was arrested late on the Thursday night and by the middle of the following afternoon he was already dead. The Sabbath Day started at sunset on the Friday, and no Jewish criminal was allowed to be left hanging on a cross after that time. In the short time between his arrest and execution he was questioned by both the Jewish and Roman authorities.

The Gospels give us different accounts of exactly what happened during the night before the death of Jesus, but it is still possible to put together a rough timetable:

Thursday 10.00 p.m.
Jesus was taken before Annas, the father-in-law of the High Priest, Caiaphas. Annas had been High Priest himself until recently, and was still regarded as the senior man by many Jews.

Thursday 11.00 p.m.
Jesus appeared before Caiaphas. A proper court hearing before the whole Sanhedrin Council could not be held until after dawn, as the Jewish law did not allow it. So Caiaphas called together some of the members of the Sanhedrin late that night for a preliminary interview with Jesus. There were important questions to be answered:

What did the High Priest traditionally do to his robes to express his deep sorrow?

- Had Jesus broken the Jewish law? No!

- Were the healing acts of Jesus on Shabbat (the Sabbath Day) against the law? No!

- Had Jesus spoken clear **blasphemy** against God? No!

- Could the witnesses against Jesus agree amongst themselves? No!

Finally, one last trap was set to catch Jesus. *'Are you the Messiah, the Son of the beloved God?'*, Caiaphas asked him. *'The words are yours'*, replied Jesus. It is not clear what he meant by this, but Caiaphas took it to be an admission of guilt and tore his own robes. The Council members agreed that it was blasphemous for anyone to claim to be God – and they considered that this was what Jesus had just done.

Friday 4.00 a.m.
Jesus was taken before the Sanhedrin council. Shortly after dawn the full Sanhedrin council of 71 members met to condemn Jesus. Again they asked him the direct question, *'Are you the Messiah, the Son of God?'*. Jesus admitted that he was God's Messiah. In the eyes of the Sanhedrin this made him clearly guilty of blasphemy – a crime punishable by death under Jewish law. However, rather than take responsibility for putting him to death, the Sanhedrin sent Jesus to the Roman govenor of the province, Pontius Pilate.

Friday 6.00 a.m.
The Jews knew that the best time to see Pilate was early in the morning. They also knew that Pilate would not be concerned with the purely 'religious' crime of blasphemy. The charge against Jesus, therefore, was changed. In front of Pilate he was accused of:

- misleading the Jewish people.

- telling the people not to pay their taxes.

- claiming to be a leader of the Jews – the Messiah – and, therefore, being a threat to the Romans.

Pilate questioned Jesus but soon became frustrated. He tried to avoid the problem by sending Jesus to Herod Antipas, the governor of Galilee – the area from which Jesus came, who was in Jerusalem at this time. Herod, unable to find any evidence to condemn Jesus, sent him back to Pilate. Convinced of the innocence of the prisoner before him, Pilate tried to solve the problem with an old tradition which said that each Passover he could release one prisoner chosen by the people. He hoped that the people would choose Jesus but, instead, they demanded the release of Barabbas, a convicted murderer. Pilate washed his hands in front of the people as a sign that he took no further responsibility for the matter. He then handed Jesus over to his army to be crucified.

For your dictionary

Blasphemy is the crime of saying things which are thought to be offensive to God.

- Before which Jewish leader was Jesus taken when he was first arrested?
- Why was Jesus not taken before the Sanhedrin council until early on the Friday morning?
- What part did Pontius Pilate play, according to the Gospels, in the condemnation of Jesus?

You can clearly see the name of Pontius Pilate on this inscription. Try and find out ten pieces of information about him.

 a Make two copies of the Summons Sheet below. Complete the details on one sheet for the appearance of Jesus before the Sanhedrin, and the other for his appearance before Pontius Pilate.

Summons Sheet
Name
Parents' names
Year of birth [approx]
Place of birth
Occupation
How and where arrested
Responsible for arrest
Appearing before
Charged with
Evidence presented
Judgement passed
Description of prisoner

b After the heading 'Description of prisoner', either draw a court artist's impression of Jesus, or write a short written description of his appearance.

2 Read Mark's account of the trial of Jesus before the Sanhedrin council (Mark 14.53–64). Then try to answer the following questions in your own words.

a What 'crime' was Jesus said to have committed?
b Of which 'crime' was Jesus finally found guilty?

How did Jesus meet his death?

Jesus was condemned to death by **crucifixion**. This was an extremely painful way to die. It was the Roman method of execution reserved for all condemned criminals in their Empire who were not Roman citizens. Roman criminals were put to death by a much quicker method of beheading with the sword.

The road to Golgotha

After he had been condemned to death, Jesus was flogged 39 times by Roman soldiers using a whip. Like every other condemned criminal, he was then expected to carry part of his cross some 400 yards to the place of execution. Criminals were usually crucified on a hill called Golgotha which was just outside the city of Jerusalem. The Romans always executed criminals on a high hill. Can you guess why they did this?

The Gospels tell us that Jesus had been so weakened by his flogging that he collapsed on the way to Golgotha. They also record that a bystander, Simon from Cyrene in Africa, was ordered to carry Jesus' cross for the remainder of the journey to Golgotha. This journey took them along the street in Jerusalem which is now called the Via Dolorosa (the Street of Sorrows). Why do you think this name is particularly appropriate?

The death of Jesus

Once at Golgotha, Jesus was nailed and strapped to his cross before being left to die. Crucifixion was normally a slow, agonising way to die, in full view of everyone. It could take as long as a week for the victim to die, although death usually came within 24 hours. However, in the case of Jesus, the process was to be much shorter.

The Gospels tell us that Jesus was left hanging on the cross from 9 o'clock in the morning until 3 o'clock in the afternoon – a total of six hours. Towards the end of that time a soldier offered him a sponge soaked in wine to drink to lessen the pain, but Jesus refused it. During the whole time Jesus spoke just seven times. Why do you think that the words of Jesus spoken from the cross were considered to be so important by the early Christians?

Death on the cross, when it came, was from suffocation. To hasten death, the legs of the prisoner were often broken. Because Jesus died quickly, his legs were not broken. But to make sure that he was dead, a Roman soldier thrust a spear into his side. Blood and water spurted from the wound. Once again Roman justice had been ruthlessly and expertly applied. Another prisoner had been executed. Jesus was dead.

What do you think this banner tells us about Jesus' death on the cross?

- What was the name of the place where Jesus was executed and what did the name mean?
- Who was made to carry part of the cross for Jesus to the place of execution?
- What was unusual about the death of Jesus on the cross?

1 **a** Write your own short description of an execution by crucifixion.

   b The picture on the right shows a modern painting of the crucifixion of Jesus. What do you think the artist was trying to show in this picture?

2 A notice written in 3 different languages (Hebrew, Latin and Greek) was placed over the head of Jesus as he hung on the cross, on the orders of Pontius Pilate. You can see here what the inscription said in Latin: 'Rex Iudaeorum', meaning 'The King of the Jews'.

REX IUDAEORUM

a Why do you think that Pontius Pilate ordered this to be placed over the head of Jesus on the cross?
b What do you think he meant by it?
c Why do you think it was written in three different languages?

	Words spoken by Jesus on the cross	Bible reference	Spoken to …
1	"Father, forgive them; they do not know what they are doing."	Luke 23.34	
2	"I promise you that you will be with me today in Paradise."	Luke 23.43	
3	"Here is your son… here is your mother."	John 19.26–27	
4	"My God, my God why did you abandon me?"	Mark 15.34	
5	"I am thirsty."	John 19.28	
6	"It is finished!"	John 19.30	
7	"Father, into your hands I commend my spirit."	Luke 23.46	

3 **a** The table on the right is a list of the seven last things spoken by Jesus on the cross. Make a copy of this table in your exercise book, and complete the last column by looking up each reference.

b These are the only recorded words of Jesus on the cross. What do they suggest to you about his state of mind as death drew near?

What happened after the death of Jesus?

Most Christians believe that three days after his death, Jesus was brought back to life by God. This event is called the **Resurrection** and is a very important part of the Christian faith. The Gospels tell us that after appearing several times to his disciples, Jesus disappeared from the earth altogether and was taken up into heaven.

Three days after the death of Jesus

This is what seems to have happened after the death of Jesus.

Friday

Within six hours of being nailed to a Roman cross, Jesus was dead. This was an exceptionally quick death for a crucifixion and surprised everyone. The body had to be taken down from the cross straight away, since the Jewish Sabbath Day started at dusk. It was hurriedly wrapped in linen strips and laid in an unused rock tomb – like the one in the photograph.

According to the Gospels, the tomb in which the body of Jesus was laid belonged to a Jewish leader who was also a secret follower of Jesus. His name was Joseph of Arithmathea.

How would you have tried to make sure that no one stole the body of Jesus from the tomb?

Saturday

The Romans were afraid that someone might steal the body of Jesus, and so were persuaded by the Jewish leaders to place a guard outside the tomb. If anyone was going to steal the body of Jesus, who do you think would be most likely to do so, and why? Think about this carefully.

Sunday

Three of the women who were followers of Jesus were at the tomb early since, traditionally, it was their responsibility to anoint the body with spices and ointments. They were amazed to find that the tomb was unguarded, and the stone that had been used to seal the entrance had been rolled away. An angel appeared to them and told them that Jesus had risen from the dead, as he had promised. When the women told the disciples in Jerusalem what they had seen they did not believe it. Peter and John went to the tomb to find only the linen wrappings in which the body of Jesus had been buried.

Why do you think that the rising of Jesus from the dead became so important for all Christians? What did it tell them?

Who saw Jesus?

Was the Resurrection of Jesus just wishful thinking? Could the disciples of Jesus have just looked in the wrong tomb? Did someone steal the body and pretend that he had risen from the dead? Were the disciples imagining it all, or did too many people see Jesus after the Resurrection for there to be any doubt? Think about what happened:

- Mary Magdalene, the first person to see Jesus alive, did not recognise him at first.
- Two disciples (we do not know who) met Jesus when they were walking from Jerusalem to Emmaus but they failed for some time to recognise who their companion was.
- Jesus made several 'appearances' to his disciples, and on one occasion he invited 'doubting' Thomas to touch his wounds to prove he was indeed risen from the dead.

What do you make of the fact that many of those who first saw Jesus did not recognise him? Does the fact that Jesus only appeared to his own followers, and not to anyone else, surprise you?

How can we explain the Resurrection?

What can we make of all this? It would seem that the opponents of Jesus were not able to solve that mystery – although they would have liked to! If anyone had been able to produce the body of Jesus, the faith of the early Christians would have been a laughing stock. The Resurrection was as important as that!

 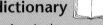
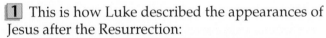

- What is the name given to the Christian belief that Jesus came back from the dead?
- In whose tomb was the body of Jesus laid?
- According to the Gospels, who was the first person to see Jesus alive?

What happened on the road from Jerusalem to Emmaus soon after Jesus had risen from the dead?

1 This is how Luke described the appearances of Jesus after the Resurrection:

'For forty days after his death he showed himself to them many times, in ways that proved beyond doubt that he was alive; he was seen by them and talked with them about the Kingdom of God.' (Acts 1.3)

Do you think the most likely explanation is that Jesus did indeed rise from the dead, or can you think of any other explanations?

2 The Gospel references below are all accounts relating to Jesus' resurrection. Copy the table below into your exercise book. Look up each of these references and sum up, in one sentence, the event described.

Bible reference	Event described
Matthew 28.1–10	
Matthew 28.16–20	
Mark 16.1–8	
Luke 24.1–12	
Luke 24.13–35	
Luke 24.36–53	
John 20.1–10	
John 21.1–14	
John 21.15–24	

3 In his novel *The Davidson Affair* Stuart Jackman imagines a television interview with Pontius Pilate by an interviewer called Tennel:

Tennel: The rumour, is, sir, that he is alive again.

Pilate: Alive again? Oh come now, Mr Tennel, really…

Tennel: Still alive, then, put it that way…

Pilate: Mr Tennel, he was executed by soldiers of the Tenth Legion. They're not amateurs, you know. When they kill a man he's dead and stays dead.

a What alternative explanations have you come up with for the missing body of Jesus? What are the arguments for and against each of your alternatives?
b Why would Pontius Pilate have been unhappy if Jesus had still been alive?

4 Copy the table below into your book. Write a brief account of what each of these eye-witnesses saw after the resurrection of Jesus.

Eye-witness	What did they see?
Mary Magdalene	
Two disciples on the road to Emmaus	
Peter and John	
Thomas	

The history of the Christian Church
What happened on the Day of Pentecost?

Most of our information about the first followers of Jesus comes from the book which comes after the four Gospels in the New Testament – the Acts of the Apostles. It was written by one of the Gospel writers – Luke, a doctor and a friend of Paul. It charts the early days and months of the Christian Church after Jesus left the earth. It begins with the Day of Pentecost – the day on which the Christian Church was born.

How is the Holy Spirit represented on this banner? Why is this particular symbol chosen? What do you think the symbol represents?

The Holy Spirit

Jesus appeared to his followers many times in the forty days which followed his Resurrection from the dead. Then one day, in the presence of his **apostles**, he simply disappeared – never to be seen again! Before leaving them, however, Jesus told them to wait in Jerusalem for a 'gift' – the gift of the Holy Spirit. He said:

'When the Holy Spirit comes upon you, you will be filled with power, and you will be witnesses for me in Jerusalem, in all Judea and Samaria, and to the ends of the earth.' (Acts 1.8)

The apostles did as they were told and, according to Luke, an extraordinary event took place. You can read Luke's account in Exercise 1.

Understanding Pentecost

How can we understand what happened at Pentecost? Did it really happen just as Luke describes it? Is Luke's account simply a way of describing the moment when the apostles lost their fear of telling others about Jesus? Perhaps it is a way of describing the inner spiritual or emotional experience of the apostles? What do you think? Perhaps the most satisfactory answer is that we simply do not know. What is plain, however, is that the apostles were never the same again and there must have been some reason why!

What did other people think had happened? Luke goes on to say that a large crowd gathered outside the house because of all the noise of the apostles speaking in other languages. Many of the crowd had travelled to Jerusalem from other countries for the festival of Passover. They were astonished to hear their own languages being spoken. This is how Luke describes their reaction:

'These people who are talking like this are Galileans! How is it then that all of us hear them speaking in our own native languages…about the great things God has done.' (Acts 2.7,11)

For your dictionary

The word **apostle** comes from the Greek word 'to send' and was used as a title for the disciples after the Resurrection of Jesus.

The spreading of the Christian message

The people who listened and responded took the Christian Gospel home with them. Already the message was beginning to spread through the Roman Empire.

However, not everyone responded, or believed what had happened to the apostles on the day of Pentecost. There were those who said '*These people are drunk*'. Peter, the leader of the apostles, told them that it was far too early in the day for anyone to be drunk. Instead, he explained, the Spirit of God had been given to them. Peter went on to tell the crowd what he and the other Christians believed. He challenged his listeners to believe what he was telling them, to turn away from their sin, to be baptised and 'receive' the Holy Spirit. In the Acts of the Apostles, Luke reports that about 3,000 people believed, and were baptised, on the Day of Pentecost alone.

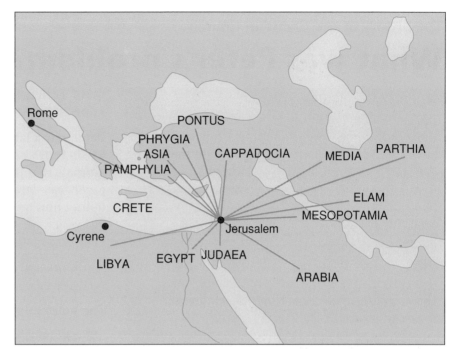

Why were the people from these areas important for the early spread of Christianity?

- From where do we get our information about the Early Church?
- What 'gift' was given to the apostles on the Day of Pentecost?
- What else happened on the Day of Pentecost?

1 This is how Luke describes what happened on the Day of Pentecost:

'*The Day of Pentecost had come, and they were all together in one place. Suddenly there came from the sky what sounded like a strong, driving wind, a noise which filled the whole house where they were sitting. And there appeared to them flames like tongues of fire distributed among them and coming to rest on each one. They were all filled with the Holy Spirit.*' (Acts 2.1–4)

Think yourself back to the Day of Pentecost and imagine that you are one of the apostles on that morning.
a Describe briefly in your own words how you might have felt, *or*
b Act out the events of the morning of Pentecost in your class and make a tape of your performance, *or*
c Draw your impression of the scene.

2 What do *you* think really happened to the apostles on the Day of Pentecost? Imagine that you had been present. Write a letter to a friend describing what actually took place – as you saw it.

What was Peter's problem?

Do you remember Simon Peter? Well, he had a problem after the Resurrection of Jesus and the birth of the Christian Church. As the most prominent of the disciples, he found himself as the leader of the Christian communiy. The members of that community were all Jews who had become followers of Jesus. No Gentile could be a member of the Christian community.

If this state of affairs had been allowed to continue, then Christianity would have become little more than an off-shoot of the Jewish religion. However, within a short time the situation changed dramatically.

Many Christians leave Jerusalem

The Jewish leaders rejected everything that the Christians claimed about Jesus, just as they had rejected the teachings of Jesus himself. Relations between the Christian Jews and the other Jews grew steadily worse. The Christians no longer found themselves welcome in the Jewish places of worship. Afraid, many Christians left Jerusalem. You can find out where they went by looking at the map on the right.

Those Christians who remained in Jerusalem tried to stay faithful to both their Jewish background and their new-found Christian faith. They continued to follow the many Jewish rules about what they should eat, about cleanliness and what they should wear. One of these rules concerned contact with Gentiles – any contact was strictly forbidden. This was Peter's problem. As a good Jew he believed that all Christians should follow the old Jewish laws – until something happened to make him change his mind.

Peter's vision

The problem for the young Christian community was straightforward – at least in theory. Did Jesus come to help everyone or just the Jews? Peter's opinion on the issue changed when a Gentile Roman soldier, Cornelius, sent messengers to him in Joppa asking Peter to visit his home in Caesarea.

Peter would normally have turned down the invitation. However, something happened to Peter in Joppa which changed his whole attitude to the Christian Gospel. Whether it took place in his own mind, or whether it really happened, we do not know. It happened like this:

Peter saw a large sheet being lowered from heaven by its four corners, in which were held all the animals that Jews were not allowed to eat. But Peter was very hungry, and when he heard a voice telling him to kill and eat he was very tempted. However, he recoiled in horror because he was a very good and proud Jew. He said:

'Certainly not, Lord. No forbidden or defiled food has ever entered my mouth.' (Acts 10.14)

The voice told him off:

'Do not consider anything to be unclean that God has declared clean.' (Acts 10.15)

To underline this the vision, or dream, returned three times!

Shortly after this, three messengers arrived from Cornelius. Peter was told by the Holy Spirit to give them a warm welcome, and before long he was travelling back with them to Caesarea.

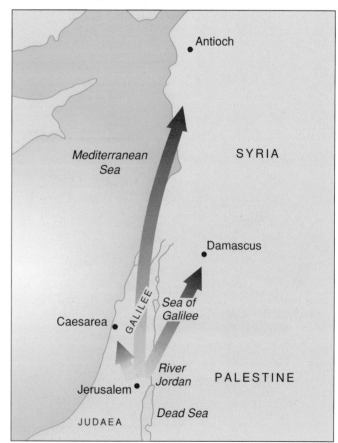

Why did the early Christians leave Jerusalem?

Through his dream God had shown Peter that all people, whether Jews or Gentiles, were equal. God had no favourites. You can read for yourself in Acts 10.34–43 what Peter told Cornelius when he arrived.

Then, just as on the Day of Pentecost, the Holy Spirit was given, but this time it was to the Gentiles. From now on the Christian faith would be open to everyone.

- Why did so many Christians leave Jerusalem?
- What event changed Peter's mind about the Gentiles?
- What did Peter learn about God from his experience?

These refugees leave the battle-ground of Yugoslavia in 1992 clutching just a few belongings. How do you think the early Christians felt as they were forced to leave their homes in Jerusalem?

1 Use the following information to write a description, in about 200 words, of Peter.

- Originally called Simon. Name changed by Jesus to Peter ('the rock').

- The only disciple of Jesus known to have been married.

- After the death of Jesus he led the Christian Church in Jerusalem for 20 years.

- Roman Catholics believe that he was the first Bishop of Rome and the predecessor of all Popes.

- Probably died by being crucified upside down by Emperor Nero in 62 CE.

2 Things that Peter **could not** eat

Things that Peter **could** eat

These Jewish food laws are known as kosher ('fit'). They are based on laws given by God to Moses and recorded in Leviticus, Chapter 11.
a Which of these animals were held in the sheet in Peter's vision?
b Why did Peter not want to eat them, as the voice ordered?
c What did Peter say in reply?
d What did Peter learn from the conversation?

Who was Saul of Tarsus?

Early in the Acts of the Apostles Luke tells us that a man named Saul looked after the coats of the people as they stoned **Stephen**, the first Christian to die for his faith. Saul was a member of the strict group of Jews called Pharisees, and he believed that all Christians should be rooted out and destroyed. Why do you think that Saul was so keen to put to death as many Christians as possible?

On the road to Damascus

Saul was certainly determined in his hunt for those who belonged to the newly-founded Christian Church. You can follow his progress on the map in on page 54 as he made his way from Tarsus to Caesarea and Jerusalem, trying hard to destroy the Christians before they really gained a foothold. However, on the road to Damascus something happened which was to change the whole course of his life.

In the Acts of the Apostles, Luke gives us three separate, and slightly different, accounts of the event. Here is the first of these accounts:

'While he was still on the road and nearing Damascus suddenly a light from the sky flashed around him. He fell to the ground and heard a voice saying, 'Saul, Saul, why are you persecuting me?' 'Tell me, Lord,' he said, 'who are you?' The voice answered, 'I am Jesus, whom you are persecuting. But, now, get up and go into the city and you will be told what you have to do.' Meanwhile the men who were travelling with him stood speechless; they heard the voice but they could see no one.' (Acts 9.3–7)

Is there anything in this account that particularly surprises you? Do you think that Saul really heard a voice speaking to him, or was it something that he heard within himself? Do you think was significant that Saul's companions heard the voice but did not see anyone? Did Saul see anything?

What happened to Saul on the road to Damascus?

Saul's conversion

We do not know what really happened on the Damascus road. All we can be sure about is that Saul stopped persecuting the Christians and joined their community. It was hardly surprising that many of the Christians found this hard to believe, and it was some time before Saul, or Paul as he was later known, became fully accepted as a member of the Christian community. With a past like his that was hardly surprising. However, he gradually managed to convince even the most suspicious of the Christians that he was a changed man and ready to work alongside them.

Indeed, he did much more than that. He wrote many of the books in the New Testament; he travelled thousands of miles preaching the Christian message; he almost sacrificed his life on more than one occasion and he was the person responsible, more than any other, for turning Christianity into a religion for Jew and non-Jew alike.

1 Write a description, in around 200 words, of the early life of Saul, up to the time of his conversion, using the information given below and elsewhere in this unit.

Saul was:

- born in around 10 CE in Tarsus, a Roman city of Silicia (modern Turkey).

- a Roman citizen by birth.

- a devout Jew.

- a member of the strict Jewish Pharisee party.

- a tent-maker by trade.

- unmarried.

2 Imagine that you are a Christian in Damascus who has heard of Saul's conversion to Christianity. One of your relatives was put to death by Saul. You manage to gain an interview with him. What questions would you put to him to make sure that his change of life is genuine? Make a list of these questions.

- Where do we first meet Saul in the Acts of the Apostles?
- Where did the conversion (change) of Saul take place?
- What happened to Saul as a result of this experience?

3 There are three accounts of Saul's conversion in the Acts of the Apostles. The references are given in the table below. Make a larger copy of this table in your exercise book.

a Read all three accounts and complete the table by listing all the similarities and differences you notice between the three accounts.

b Can you think of any reasons for the differences between these accounts?

Reference	Similarities	Differences
Acts 9.1–9		
Acts 22.6–10		
Acts 26.12–18		

For your dictionary 📖
Stephen was the first Christian put to death for their beliefs.

What did Paul do after his conversion?

After his Damascus road experience Saul – or Paul as he came to be known in later life – disappeared from the scene for several years. We think that he spent some of this 'missing' time in the desert, preparing himself for the work ahead. Can you remember someone else who did exactly the same thing?

Paul – the missionary

In 44 CE Paul arrived in Antioch to help teach the Christians there. The following year Paul and **Barnabas** set out on a mission to travel from city to city preaching about Jesus. Few people could have guessed at the time that Paul was going to become the greatest missionary in the history of the Christian Church.

During the next fifteen years of his life Paul spent much of his time travelling throughout the eastern part of the Roman Empire telling the people that Jesus was God's Messiah. We know a great deal about his travels because Luke seems to have been with Paul on many of his journeys. The map below shows many of the places that Paul visited. Why do you think that he travelled so far to spread the Christian message?

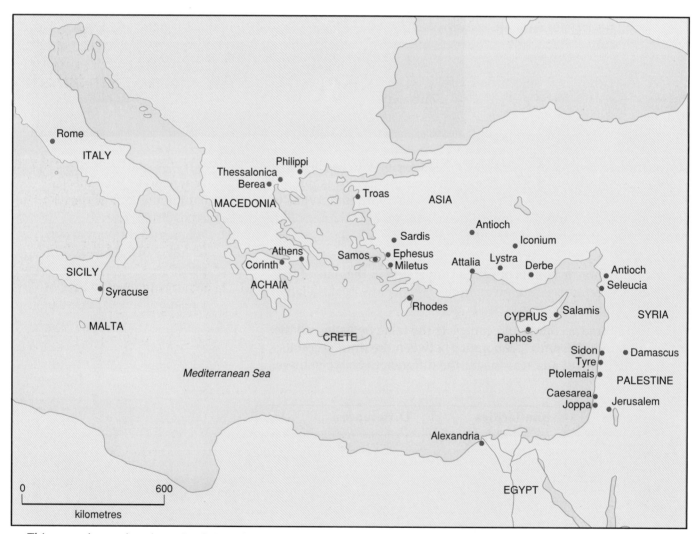

This map shows the places Paul visited on his missionary journeys. Using a piece of string and the scale on the map, work out how far Paul had to sail from Jerusalem to Rome.

The journeys of Paul were certainly eventful. Amongst other things:

- in Lystra, the people thought that Paul and Barnabas were gods and worshipped them and then, a few hours later, stoned them, dragged them out of the city and left them for dead.
- Paul was shipwrecked at least once and, quite probably, three times.
- Paul was thrown out of many cities and often put in prison for 'making trouble'.

Paul reaches Rome

In 59 CE Paul was probably getting ready to set out for Rome when he was arrested by the Romans in Jerusalem. He had always planned to preach in the Roman capital city, but events caught up with him. An angry mob attacked him, but because the Jews were determined to get rid of him they asked the Romans to find him guilty of causing the trouble. The Roman Governor refused to hand Paul over to the Jewish Council (the Sanhedrin) and sent him to prison for two years instead.

Then a new Governor was appointed and, again, the Jews tried to have Paul condemned. This time Paul revealed that he was a Roman and, as such, had the right to appeal directly to Caesar in Rome. This meant that he would have the opportunity to preach in the capital. Why do you think he wanted to preach there?

Paul was sent from Jerusalem to Rome by boat under an armed escort. It was a very dangerous journey. Luke's description of it gives us a vivid account of the dangers of sea-travel in those days. The ship was caught in a storm and the crew and passengers were shipwrecked but, in time, Paul did reach Rome. We do not know exactly what happened to him there, but it seems highly likely that he was put to death by the mad Roman Emperor, Nero, in 64 CE.

- Who looked after Paul when he was converted to Christianity?
- Which city did Paul want to reach more than any other?
- How did he reach it?

How does this photograph help you to understand how a crowd could treat Paul and Barnabas as gods and then, a few hours later, try to stone them to death?

For your dictionary
Barnabas was a Jewish Christian from Cyprus who accompanied Paul on his early missionary travels.

1 **a** Read Acts 27.1–44, Luke's account of Paul's sea voyage to Rome.

b Describe briefly in your own words each of the following events during Paul's journey:

- The difficulties encountered in the early part of the journey.
- Paul's warning against putting out to sea.
- The crew jettisoning the ship's gear.
- Paul's promise that the ship will be safe.
- The storm.
- The ship running aground.

2 Imagine that you are the captain of the ship on which Paul sailed to Rome. Write a short log of your voyage. Describe the storm as it is happening. Will you survive? What are you most afraid of? What do you think of Paul? Do you think he is afraid?

How did Christianity conquer the Roman Empire?

In the first two hundred years of its history the Christian Church survived many periods of persecution. The Roman authorities saw it as a threat because Christians refused:

1 to burn incense in front of the Emperor's statue.
2 to celebrate the Emperor's birthday, which was a public holiday in the Roman Empire.
3 to fight in the Roman army.

Can you think of any reasons why the early Christians should have refused to do these things?

Who was the first Roman Emperor to support the Christian Church?

Martyrs for the Christian faith

It was hardly surprising that the early Christians upset the Roman authorities. The Romans responded with force. For example, the Emperor Septimus Severus (193–211) made it illegal for any person to try to convert someone else to the Christian faith. Those caught trying to do so were punished, and some were even put to death. Those who died at the hands of the Romans became heroes in the Christian Church and were known as **martyrs**. The martyrs gave great courage to other Christians.

What persuaded the Emperor Constantine to become a Christian?

Christianity conquers the Roman Empire

Early in the fourth century the attitude of the Roman Emperors towards Christianity began to change. In 311 the Emperor Galerian agreed to pass a law for the toleration of Christianity. Two years later the Eastern Emperor, Licinius, and the Western Emperor, **Constantine**, met in Milan and decreed that toleration of Christianity should be the future policy of the whole Roman Empire. They stated that Christians should:

'...have liberty to follow the manner of religion they choose'

and they added that:

'...all who chose to be Christians are to be freely and totally permitted to do so, without being disturbed or in any way molested.'

Constantine himself became a Christian because he believed that the God of the Christians had given him victory in a battle against his main rival. Constantine was so sure that he had God's support that he carried a famous Christian symbol on his banner as he went into all future battles. What do you think that symbol was? You can find out by looking at the photograph on the left. Constantine was baptised as a Christian on his death-bed in 337.

Constantine founded a new capital for his Empire, Constantinople, stamped Christian symbols on his coins and built many beautiful churches. Before long, Christianity was looked upon as the state religion. Many Christians became soldiers in the Roman army. The Christian religion itself was also beginning to change. In its new form it began to reach the remotest parts of the Roman Empire.

- Why were the early Christians persecuted by the Romans?
- Who became the first Christian Roman Emperor?
- What did the Emperors Licinius and Constantine agree in Milan?

1 A Christian called Hippolytus, writing at the end of the third century, had this to say about those wanting to be baptised into the Christian Church:

'If a man is a priest of idols or a keeper of idols he must either give this up or be rejected for baptism. A soldier must be told not to execute people; even if he is ordered to do so, he must not. He must be told not to take the military oath. If he does not accept this, let him be rejected for baptism. If a baptised Christian wants to become a soldier, he must be thrown out because he has despised God.'

Imagine that you are Septimus Severus, the Roman Emperor. A copy of Hippolytus' words come into your hands. Write a few sentences to say what you would do about the Christian 'threat' to your Empire.

2 Blandina, along with other Christians, was put to death in 177 in Lyons, southern France. This is how an eyewitness described the scene of her death:

'Blandina, hanging on a stake, was offered as food to wild animals which were let loose on her. Yet when other suffering Christians saw her there, hanging crosswise and earnestly praying, they were themselves strengthened, seeing through her Jesus, who had been crucified for them.'

a How did the suffering and courage of Blandina help others?

b Here are the names of four people who have lost their lives in recent years because of their Christian faith. Find out as much as you can about *one* of them.

Dietrich Bonhoeffer   Janani Luwum

Oscar Romero   Martin Luther King

3 Here is a crossword with the answers filled in. Make up a one-sentence clue to go with each the answer.

How did Christianity reach Britain?

To most Roman citizens and soldiers, Britain seemed as far away from Rome as Australia does to us today. Yet nowhere was beyond the reach of the early Christians, who were determined to spread the Christian message everywhere. There is every reason to think that the Christian Gospel first reached Britain early in the second century.

Early missionaries

The truth of when and how Christianity first reached Britain is a mystery. Some legends tell us that Paul reached this country on one of his missionary journeys or even that Jesus himself came here. We will never know the names of the earliest Christian missionaries to Britain. It seems likely that they were soldiers sent to the furthest outpost of the Roman Empire to maintain law and order. Perhaps the best-known of these early Roman missionaries was Alban.

Who was Alban?

The execution of Alban, the first known Christian martyr to have been put to death in Britain, probably took place as early as the year 209. Alban appears to have been a Roman soldier who was caught sheltering a Christian priest who had escaped from Gaul (modern France). This much appears to be certain. The rest is only legend.

The story is that Alban was sentenced to be beheaded, but the eyes of his executioner fell out so that he would be unable to see the death of his victim. St Alban's Cathedral now stands on the spot where Alban is thought to have died.

Three later missionaries

Three missionaries in particular helped to bring Christianity to Britain and Ireland.

St Patrick

At the age of twenty Patrick, who had been born in northern England, was taken as a slave to Ireland. He was a Christian and as he looked after his new

What legend is associated with the beheading of Alban?

owner's sheep he described his feelings in the following words:

'I used to pray constantly. In a single day I said a hundred prayers. Overnight I said almost as many. Before dawn broke I would rise in snow and frost and rain and begin praying.'

Patrick escaped to France where he became a priest, but he was soon back in Ireland preaching. Soon afterwards he was made Bishop of Armagh, where he baptised thousands of Christian converts.

St Columba

Columba was an Irishman who took Christianity to Scotland. He arrived there in 563, landing on the island of Iona where he built a monastery. This monastery was rebuilt in the 1930s and is now the home of a Christian community. Columba went on to convert the pagan king, Brude, to Christianity before founding more monasteries.

St Augustine

In 596 a group of Christians were sent to England as missionaries from Rome by Pope Gregory the Great. Their leader was Augustine and when they arrived they were surprised to find a Christian Church already in existence. Amongst the first converts to the preaching of Augustine was King Ethelbert of Kent. On Christmas Day 597 Augustine baptised more than a thousand new converts. The King presented Augustine with the land on which the first cathedral at Canterbury was built. Augustine became the first Archbishop of Canterbury, and turned many of the old pagan temples into churches. In the process, however, Augustine managed to fall out with most of those who had become Christians before he arrived.

- How did the Christian message first reach Britain?
- Who was Alban and what happened to him?
- What parts did Patrick, Columba and Augustine play in spreading the Christian message to Britain and Ireland?

Can you find out why the re-opening of the Christian monastery on Iona was considered to be very important by many Christians?

1 There are many legends that people mentioned in the Bible visited Britain. Amongst these are Peter, Paul, Jesus and Joseph of Arithmathea. Many of these legends are associated with such places as Glastonbury. Find out about one such legend and write a short account of it in your exercise book.

2 The names of five saints mentioned in this unit are hidden in this wordsquare. Write two sentences about each of these saints as you find their names.

R	T	I	Y	P	A	U	L	M	N	R	Q
T	U	T	G	D	L	M	B	Q	R	P	F
V	R	T	P	K	B	M	G	J	K	L	R
B	M	T	U	Y	A	W	F	D	L	R	T
S	T	R	Y	U	N	M	B	V	R	X	A
D	P	A	T	R	I	C	K	L	T	B	N
P	I	U	P	Y	T	O	L	J	H	N	M
T	R	Y	G	H	M	L	J	A	W	Q	M
O	Y	Y	A	U	G	U	S	T	I	N	E
M	N	B	V	C	F	M	A	R	Y	T	U
D	F	G	H	J	K	B	D	W	Q	T	Y
F	G	H	J	K	L	A	J	N	V	B	L

What was the Great Schism?

Between 597 (when Augustine came to England) and 1500 the Christian Church in Europe grew much stronger. Missionaries, teachers, writers, artists, craftsmen and builders all helped the Church to establish itself. The general calm was only broken by a quarrel amongst the leaders of the Church in the eleventh century, which lead to the Church breaking up into two parts:

- the **Catholic** ('universal') **Church** with its headquarters in Rome;

- the **Orthodox** ('correct belief') **Church** centred on Constantinople (modern day Istanbul).

These two branches of the Christian Church still remain separated today, almost 1000 years later. In fact, they have only just begun talking to each other once again. This division began in 1054 with the Great Schism.

What was the argument about?

Before the eleventh century, Church leaders had increasingly disagreed among themselves about several matters. In particular, they could not agree about the authority which the Pope should have within the Church.

- The Orthodox Church was never prepared to give the Pope the sole right to determine the doctrines (beliefs) that Christians should hold.

- The Roman Catholic Church believed that the Pope was the successor of St Peter, the first Bishop of Rome. As such, his authority over the Church could not be questioned.

The two Churches also disagreed about something else. It may seem trivial now, but at the time it was considered to be of great importance. It was to do with what Christians believed about the three parts of the **Holy Trinity** – God the Father, God the Son (Jesus) and God the Holy Spirit. A very important Christian **creed**, the Nicene Creed, had said that the Holy Spirit came 'only from the Father'. The words 'God the Son' were added later and accepted by the Roman Catholic Church. The Orthodox Church never accepted this, insisting that God the Son and God the Holy Spirit both came from God the Father alone.

This disagreement led to the great division (schism) which followed.

This is the church of St Peter in Rome – the Pope's own church. Can you find out three things which Roman Catholics today believe about the Pope – and why?

The Great Schism

Michael Cerularius, head of the Orthodox Church in Constantinople, accused the Roman Catholic Church of holding false beliefs (called 'heresy'). There could be no more serious charge. Pope Leo X denied that his Church was in error and condemned the Orthodox Church in return. The Pope then died. In the same year the Papal representative, Cardinal Humbert of France, excommunicated not only Patriarch Michael of Constantinople, but also the entire Orthodox Church! This had never been done before – or since! The reaction from Constantinople was to deny that the Pope had any authority over the Orthodox Church which was, they claimed, totally independent of the Roman Catholic Church. It has remained that way ever since.

1 Cardinal Humbert excommunicated the Orthodox Church during High Mass held in the splendid Cathedral of Santa Sophia in Constantinople (shown in the photo above). He threw down the document of excommunication in front of the congregation before sweeping out of the church with the words:

'May God look upon us and judge.'

Use your imagination to write a short account or a poem in which you try to capture the pomp, surprise and atmosphere of the occasion.

For your dictionary

The **Catholic Church** traces its beginnings back to Peter who was thought to have been the first Bishop of Rome.

A **creed** is a statement of religious belief.

The **Holy Trinity** is the Christian belief that there is one God in three persons – Father, Son and Holy Spirit.

The eastern **Orthodox Church** separated from the western Catholic Church during the Great Schism of 1054.

- Which two branches of the Christian Church split from each other in 1054?
- What was the split called?
- What caused the split?

2 Using the information on this spread, copy out these sentences into your exercise book, filling in the missing words as you go:

a The _____ _____ in 1054 brought about a split between the _____ _____ and the _____ _____ .

b The _____ _____ with its headquarters in the Italian city of _____ looked upon the _____ as its supreme leader.

c Catholics believe that the Pope is the successor of _____ , the first _____ of _____ .

d Roman Catholics believed that the _____ _____ came from the _____ and the _____ as stated in the _____ _____ . The Orthodox Church believed that the _____ and the _____ _____ came from the _____ . This was the main reason for the _____ _____ .

e It was _____ _____ of _____ who finally excommunicated _____ _____ of _____ , the leader of the Orthodox Church. He did so in a service of _____ _____ in the Cathedral of _____ _____ in Constantinople.

What were the Crusades?

The seventh century saw the birth of the prophet **Muhammad** and the rapid spread of the religion of Islam. Before long it presented a real challenge to the Christian religion. By the eleventh century the Turks, who were Muslims, had conquered the holy city of Jerusalem and were threatening to attack Constantinople – the two most important Christian centres. What was the Christian response going to be?

The call to fight – in Christ's name

In 1095 Pope Urban the Second visited Clermont, in France. Whilst he was there he delivered a sermon in which he appealed for Christians everywhere to support their fellow-believers in Jerusalem who were, even at that moment, under threat from Muslim soldiers. You can read two extracts from this sermon in Exercise 1.

The Pope received an enthusiastic response. Those who set out on the First Crusade eventually reached the Holy Land and recaptured Jerusalem for Christianity. This crusade was seen by those taking part as partly a holy war, or military expedition, blessed by the Church, and partly as a pilgrimage to the Holy Land.

Does it surprise you that the Church should launch a military expedition in which so many people were killed? If so, what surprises you about it?

What happened next?

The first Crusade was only the beginning, although it was the most successful of the Crusades from a military point of view. To encourage people to go on later expeditions to the Holy Land, the Church offered incentives including:

* immunity from having to pay any taxes.

* freedom from all debts.

* protection for their own families and property at home.

* indulgences (see page 65) which guaranteed the crusader's entry into heaven and reduced the time spent in **purgatory** when they died.

It is not possible to say just how many crusades there were. The usual guess is seven or eight. In fact, after 1150, there was an almost continual movement of soldiers, pilgrims and merchants passing between Europe and the Holy Land.

Perhaps the most famous of all the crusades was

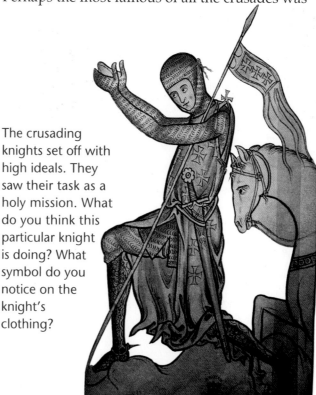

The crusading knights set off with high ideals. They saw their task as a holy mission. What do you think this particular knight is doing? What symbol do you notice on the knight's clothing?

Map labels:
NORMANDY
Clermont (Pope Urban II preaches Crusade 1095)
Toulouse
Rome
BYZANTIUM
Constantinople (Emperor appeals to Pope for help)
(Turks advance 1071–92)
Manzikert
TURKS
Nicaea (taken June 1097)
Tarsus
Antioch (taken June 1098)
Jerusalem (captured by Turks 1071; captured by Crusaders 1099)
ARABS

What was the main objective of the First Crusade? Do you think that religious people should defend, or attack, holy places using violence?

that undertaken by King Richard the First ('the Lionheart'), of England, which forms the background to many of the legends of Robin Hood. The city of Jerusalem had been lost by the Christians in 1187 but, try as hard as he might, King Richard failed to retake it.

- Which religion presented the greatest threat to Christianity in the eleventh century?
- When did the forces of the First Crusade recapture Jerusalem?
- What rewards were offered by the Church to those crusaders willing to fight to free the Holy Land?

Although the crusaders failed to achieve most of their ambitions, the military expeditions to the Holy Land rumbled on for a long time. Later, they were often directed against countries well outside the Holy Land. Their original objective was forgotten. They became an excuse for fighting and looting.

For your dictionary

Muhammad was God's messenger through whom the teachings of Islam were passed on.
Roman Catholics believe that **purgatory** is the limbo state after death for those who are not yet ready to enter heaven.

1 Here are two extracts from the sermon of Pope Urban the Second at Clermont in 1095. If you read them carefully they will give you a good idea of the strong feelings that lay behind the Crusades.

(i) From the confines of Jerusalem and from the city of Constantinople a horrible tale has gone forth. An accursed race, a race utterly alienated [cut off] from God...has invaded the lands of those Christians and depopulated them by the sword, plundering and fire.

(ii) O most valiant soldiers, descendants of invincible ancestors, be not degenerate [corrupted]. Let all hatred between you depart, all quarrels and wars cease. Start upon the road to the Holy Sepulchre, to tear that land from the wicked race and subject it to yourselves.

Imagine that you are Pope Urban the Second. Write a sermon of not more than 200 words in which you set out to move your listeners to a Holy Crusade to win back the Holy Land for Christianity.

2 At the time of the Crusades the city of Jerusalem was a holy place for three different religions. It still is. Can you find out which three religions lay claim to it?

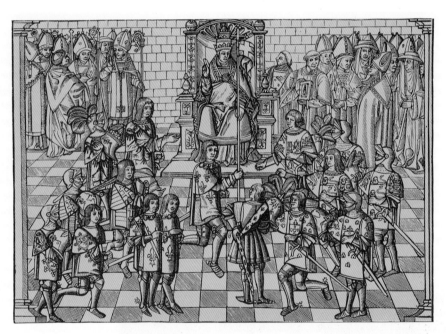

3 The following poem was written about the Crusades. Read it carefully.

'When men are hot with drinking wine
And jolly by the fire recline,
They take the cross with eager boast
To make a great crusading host.
But with the first glow of morning light
The whole Crusade dissolves in flight.'

a This poem gives several reasons why so many people responded to the call to fight in Christ's name. What are they?
b What later persuaded many people that fighting was not such a good idea after all?
c Do you think that many crusaders later regretted their decision to go and fight?

What was the Reformation?

The Christian Church had split into two parts in 1054 – the Orthodox Church and the Catholic Church. It split into many more parts during the sixteenth century, during the period known as the **Reformation**. This is one of the most important periods in the history of the Christian Church.

Martin Luther and the Catholic Church

At the beginning of the sixteenth century, a German monk called Martin Luther, who was a Catholic, became unhappy about the Church, and about the behaviour of many Catholic priests. Luther believed that the rulers of the Church were out of touch with the needs of ordinary people. They were rich and openly enjoyed the luxuries that money could buy. Ordinary people were angry that they were being forced to give money to the Church, and that this was sent to Rome and wasted on luxury.

At the very time when this anger and dissatisfaction was growing, Pope Leo X demanded yet more money to rebuild St Peter's Church in Rome. To persuade people to give, he granted an **indulgence** to anyone who gave money towards the rebuilding. Those too old to pay could obtain an indulgence simply by saying their prayers. Why do you think that Luther, and others, objected so strongly to this way of raising money for the Church?

This photograph shows a Jesuit priest at work. Why was the Jesuit order founded?

Priests travelled from Rome to Germany to preach, sell the indulgences and raise money. Martin Luther said that this was wrong, and by doing this upset his superiors. The Pope ordered him to change his views and summoned him to a special meeting in the town of Worms in 1521. You can read what Luther had to say at this meeting in Exercise 3.

People throughout Germany took sides in the quarrel. Many broke away from the Catholic Church and formed their own Protestant Churches. Why do you think they were given this name? This splitting from the Catholic Church was known as the Reformation.

Many Roman Catholics tried to reform the bad practices in their own Church rather than leaving it. During the period known as the **Counter-Reformation** a missionary society called 'The Society of Jesus' was formed in 1540. This was later known as the Jesuits. The founder of the Jesuits was Ignatius of Loyola and the society is still continuing its work today.

The Reformation in England

Protestant Churches were soon being formed in other countries throughout Europe. These Churches no longer accepted the authority of the Catholic Church or the Pope in Rome. Instead they appointed their own leaders. A Frenchman, John Calvin, formed a Protestant Church in Geneva and 'Calvinistic' Churches were started in France and the Netherlands. The French Protestants were called Huguenots.

In England, King Henry VIII had a bitter dispute with the Pope over whether he could divorce his wife, Catherine of Aragon. Eventually the King broke away from the Catholic Church in Rome. He himself became head of the English Church (later called the Church of England) just as the present Queen still is today.

- Which German monk was unhappy with the Roman Catholic Church?
- Which Roman Catholic practice upset him the most?
- Which English king broke the link between the Church in England and the Catholic Church in Rome?

1 Use the information given below and on this spread to write a few sentences about Martin Luther.

Martin Luther…

- was born on 10 December 1483.

- was the son of a German mine owner.

- entered a monastery of the Order of St Augustine of Hippo at the age of 22.

- was appointed as a teacher at the University of Wittenburg in 1509.

- published a document in Wittenburg in 1517 against the practice of selling indulgences, and this began the Reformation.

- married Katherine Von Bera in 1525.

- died on 15 February 1546.

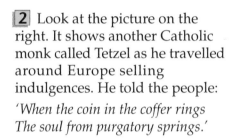

2 Look at the picture on the right. It shows another Catholic monk called Tetzel as he travelled around Europe selling indulgences. He told the people:

*'When the coin in the coffer rings
The soul from purgatory springs.'*

Why do you think that these words made Martin Luther so angry?

3 Martin Luther made the following statement to the Church council at Worms in 1521. Read it carefully and then answer the questions below.

'I am bound by the Scripture. My conscience is captive to the Word of God. I neither can nor will revoke anything. It is neither safe nor honest to act against one's conscience.'

a Luther uses two other names for the Bible. What are they?
b What two reasons does Luther give for his unwillingness to go back on anything he has said?
c What is meant by 'acting against one's conscience'?
d Why do you think that Martin Luther believed that it was neither safe nor honest to act against one's conscience?

For your dictionary

The **Counter-Reformation** was the movement for reform within the Catholic Church in response to the Protestant Reformation.
Indulgences were pardons granted by the Catholic Church in return for payment. They pardoned the giver from punishment for their sins.
The Protestant **Reformation** began with Martin Luther's actions in Wittenburg in 1517.

How did the Church face new challenges?

In time, the Protestant Church itself broke up into many smaller Churches. Starting with the **Methodist Church** in the eighteenth century, a whole succession of smaller Churches were established. They were called **Nonconformist Churches** because they refused to 'conform' to the teachings of the Church of England.

Methodism

John Wesley did not intend to start a new branch of the Christian Church, but that is what happened after his death in 1791. Whilst at Oxford University the two Wesley brothers – John and Charles – had started a 'Holy Club' (also known as the 'methodists' after their methodical way of studying the Bible together). This became the name of the new Christian denomination based on Wesley's teaching.

John Wesley preaching whilst standing on his father's grave in Epworth churchyard. How did the Methodists get their name?

In May 1738 John Wesley, whose father was a Church of England vicar, had a spiritual experience which convinced him that he would be saved through trusting in Christ. Soon afterwards he began to travel the country on horseback with his brother preaching the Christian message. Bristol, Newcastle-upon-Tyne and Macclesfield became the main centres of the new Methodism. Wesley also travelled to America as well as Scotland and Ireland. Indeed, it is estimated that this travelling preacher covered at least 250,000 miles and preached 40,000 sermons in his lifetime. He was 81 years old when he preached his last sermon – at Winchelsea in Sussex.

The nineteenth century

During the nineteenth century, Christians were prominent in the struggles for much-needed social reform. Amongst them were:

William Wilberforce who led the fight against the African slave trade.

The Earl of Shaftsbury who fought for the banning of all child labour.

Elizabeth Fry, a Quaker, who worked to improve the conditions of people in prison.

William Booth who fought against the evils of drink and founded the Salvation Army in 1864.

Thomas Barnardo who founded a society to look after homeless children.

The twentieth century

In the twentieth century there have been many Christians who have devoted themselves to helping the poor and the needy. Toyohito Kagawa dedicated his life to helping the sick and unemployed in the slums of Japanese towns before his death in 1960. Dr Albert Schweitzer, a German, spent most of his long life helping the sick in Africa. Martin Luther King, a Baptist minister, was assassinated in 1968 after opposing racial hatred in America. Mother

Theresa, an Albanian Catholic nun, has become world-famous for her work amongst the poor in Calcutta and other cities.

There has also been a deep desire to overcome the many divisions which separate the different Churches. There are currently well over 10,000 different Churches worldwide. The World Council of Churches (WCC), formed in 1948, is a fellowship of more than 200 different Churches which:

'…confess the Lord Jesus Christ as their God and Saviour according to the Scriptures and therefore seek to fulfil their common calling to the glory of one God, Father, Son and Holy Spirit.'

Membership of the WCC includes most of the Churches of the great Christian traditions – Protestant, Anglican and Orthodox – although not, as yet, the Roman Catholic Church.

- Which new Christian Church was formed after the death of John Wesley?
- In which areas of life did prominent Christians work in the nineteenth century?
- What is the World Council of Churches?

For your dictionary

The Methodist Church is a Protestant Christian denomination based on the preaching of John Wesley.
Nonconformist Churches are Protestant Churches which do not belong to the Church of England.

1 Find out all that you can about *one* of the outstanding nineteenth-century Christians mentioned on this spread or about another Christian of the nineteenth or twentieth century who made a real impact because of their faith.

2 This is the symbol of the World Council of Churches. Like most symbols it carries a great deal of information. Find out:
a what the word 'Oikumene' means.
b why a cross stands at the centre of the symbol.
c why the symbol includes a boat sailing on the water.

3 St Augustine of Hippo once said:
'In essentials – unity. In areas of doubt – freedom. In all things – charity.'

a Try to explain what you think he meant by these words.
b How do you think these words might apply to Christian unity?

4 In his journal, Wesley describes the spiritual experience that led him to begin his mission:
'About a quarter before nine oclock, while he [a visiting preacher] was describing the change God works in the heart through faith in Christ, I felt my heart strangely warmed. I felt that I did trust in Christ, Christ alone for my salvation; and an assurance was given me that He had taken away my sins, even mine, and saved me from the law of sin and death.'

a Why do you think that Wesley dates this experience so precisely – 'about a quarter before nine oclock'?
b What do you think the visiting preacher was telling the people?
c What do you think Wesley meant by the words 'I felt my heart strangely warmed'?

4 The Bible
What's in the Bible?

The Bible is the holy book for all Christians. The word 'Bible' comes from a Greek word meaning 'the books'. That is an important clue to understanding what the Bible is. The Bible is not *one* book at all – it is a collection of many books brought together.

The Bible as a collection

The Bible that most people use today contains 66 books written by many different authors over a long period of thousands of years. These books include history, stories, fables, poetry, songs, parables, laws, sermons, letters and predictions about the future. To have all those in one book must be unique! On this spread you will see a diagram of the Bible Library. From this you will be able to see the different categories into which the different books of the Bible belong. The Bible is divided into two parts – the Old and New Testaments.

The Old Testament

Stories and story-telling play an important part in almost all religions. The stories of the Old Testament, the Holy Bible for all Jews, were kept alive for centuries by word of mouth (called the **Oral Tradition**). Centuries later these stories were written down on tablets of clay although, as you can imagine, these were very difficult to carry from place to place. Often they were broken. We are told, for instance, that Moses recorded the famous **Ten Commandments** on tablets of stone – and then had to stagger down a mountainside carrying them. It was not long before they were both broken – but that's another story!

The Old Testament describes events that took place in the centuries before the coming of Christ. Covering a period of almost 2,000 years, it is the story of the nation of Israel and its people – the Israelites or Hebrews. The Israelites believed that they had a special relationship with God (they were sometimes called 'The Chosen People') which God proved when he led them out of slavery in Egypt towards the Promised Land of Canaan. The journey that they took, called the **Exodus**, is the most important event in Jewish history. Jews celebrate the journey each year with the festival of Pesach (see page 36).

The New Testament

There are 27 books in the New Testament, all written in the 100 years or so following the death of Jesus. Two centuries later, the Christian Church gathered these books together and placed them alongside the Jewish Scriptures (the Old Testament) to form the Bible that we know today.

Almost our entire knowledge of Jesus and the early Christian Church comes from the New Testament. It contains three different kinds of books:

- **Epistles** or letters. The earliest known Christian writings are those written by Paul (see page 52). A total of 14 letters in the New Testament carry Paul's name, although he certainly did not write all of them. Others were written by Peter, John, James and Jude.

The Bible Library

Copy this chart into your book.

The Books of the Law
The first five books of the Bible are called the **Pentateuch** or 'the five books of the scroll'. The Pentateuch contains the early history of Israel, including the stories of Abraham and Moses, and God's law for Israel, including the Ten Commandments. Jews call these books 'the Books of the Law' or the **Torah**.

GENESIS EXODUS LEVITICUS NUMBERS DEUTERONOMY

Old Testament

New Testament

- Gospels and the Acts of the Apostles. There are four Gospels in all (see page 6). The Acts of the Apostles (see page 48) tells us how the belief that Jesus had risen from the dead changed the disciples from frightened cowards into powerful preachers.

- The Book of Revelation. Written in a kind of code towards the end of the first century, the Book of Revelation was intended to encourage the Christians who were being persecuted by speaking about the end of the world.

- What was the Exodus?
- What are the earliest known Christian writings?
- Which book in the New Testament tells us about the history of the early Christian Church?

For your dictionary

The **Epistles** are letters included in the New Testament and written by Paul, Peter and John, among others.

The **Exodus** was the journey of the Israelites out of slavery in Egypt.

By way of the **Oral Tradition**, many stories in the Bible were kept alive by word of mouth before they were finally written down.

The **Pentateuch** are the first five books of the Bible.

The **Psalms** are a collection of songs used in Jewish worship and included in the Old Testament.

The **Ten Commandments** were part of the code of laws which, Jews believe, were given by God to Moses on Mount Sinai.

The **Torah** is the Jewish Books of the Law – the first five books of the Old Testament.

The History Books
These books tell the history of Israel from the story of Joshua leading the Israelites into the Promised Land to the defeat of the Babylonians and Persians.

Poetry and Wisdom
Whilst Job is a book about suffering, the **Psalms** are a collection of songs used in religious worship. Proverbs and Ecclesiastes bring together many wise sayings, whilst the Song of Songs is a love poem.

The Prophets
The last 17 books of the Old Testament are called 'The Prophets'. Prophets were messengers sent by God and these books record their messages to the people.

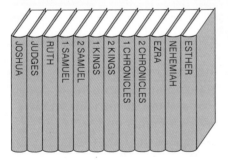

A Prophecy
Written in poetry and picture-language, the Book of Revelation is about the end of the world.

New Testament History
The first four books of the New Testament are the 'Gospels' or 'Good News'. They record the birth, life, teaching and death of Jesus. Luke, who wrote one of the Gospels, also wrote the Acts of the Apostles, the story of the early Church in the Roman Empire.

The Letters
A collection of 21 letters written by the early Christian leaders, but mainly by Paul.

Where did the Bible come from?

Where did the Old and New Testaments come from in the first place? Did God dictate them book by book to willing men and women who copied them down? Did authors sit down and write them, book by book, just as writers do today? Neither of these explanations is very satisfactory. The process by which the Bible came into being was actually very complicated.

How was the Old Testament put together?

It is not easy to discover how the books of the Old Testament came to be written as some of them are very old indeed. We can, however, piece together the most likely sequence of events:

1 Important stories were passed down for centuries by word of mouth before they were written down.

2 It then became the habit to write things down and store the material in a special place. Moses was told by God:

'Write this on a scroll as something to be remembered.'

The priests then kept the scroll beside the covenant box or Ark in the holy inner sanctuary of the Temple. The Ten Commandments were carved on small tablets of stone (about 50 cms by 30 cms) and kept in the same place.

3 From the time of **Samuel** onwards, the words of the prophets were recorded by their followers.

4 Religious songs or Psalms were probably started by King David for use in Temple worship. There are 150 Psalms in the Bible.

5 By the fifth century BCE, in the time of Ezra and Nehemiah, the Pentateuch was complete. It was the military leader Judas Maccabeus who finally brought all of the books together and arranged them under the headings of the Law, the Prophets and the Writings. By the time of Jesus there was no dispute over the writings of the Old Testament. They were formally accepted at the Synod of Jamnia in 90 CE.

How was the New Testament put together?

We have thousands of manuscripts which go back to the early years of Christianity. Through them we are able to trace just how the New Testament was put together.

- Jesus did not write a book nor did the disciples travel around with notebooks! After his death, stories about Jesus were kept alive by word of mouth. Whenever groups of Christians met, as they frequently did, they read the Jewish Scriptures together and listened to stories about Jesus from eyewitnesses, particularly the disciples.

- The first written documents in the New Testament were penned from 49 CE onwards. These were the letters, or Epistles, that Paul sent to friends and churches.

- One by one the eye-witnesses to Jesus began to die and the need to write down their information became urgent. Mark, with the help of Peter, led the way followed by Luke, Matthew and John. Luke also added his history of the early Christian Church – the Acts of the Apostles.

- Gradually, other documents were added as suitable for public reading in church. Two Christian councils in the fourth century agreed on which books should and should not be in the New Testament.

The Old and New Testaments were joined and the Bible was complete.

For your dictionary

Samuel was the last of the Israelite judges who anointed Saul and David as kings of Israel.

- How were many of the oldest stories in the New Testament passed on for centuries?
- Why were the Psalms first written?
- Which books are the oldest in the New Testament?

Which two different books are combined in the Bible that these young people from South America are reading?

1 Nehemiah, a writer in the Old Testament, is said to have founded:

'a library, gathered together the books about the kings and the prophets, and the books of David, and the letters of kings about sacred gifts.'

a What might the books about kings and prophets refer to?
b What could the books of David have been?

2 Most of you will be familiar with the game of Chinese whispers. Decide who in your class will begin the game by passing on this message:

John has bought a new personal stereo from Anne but Alan wants to borrow it for the weekend as he is going on a four-hour coach journey to Manchester.

Pass the message around the whole class until it reaches the last person. How does the message at the end compare with the one you started with? Write a few sentences to say how this could be used to explain the differences between the various Gospel accounts of the same event.

3 Ask an elderly person you know to tell you about some memories from their childhood.

a Do you think that their memories are accurate or not?
b Does it matter whether these memories are strictly accurate?
c What do other people in your class think?
d How could you apply these findings to the way that material was passed down from generation to generation before being recorded in the Bible?

Whose Bible is it anyway?

We are used to thinking of the Bible as containing the Old and New Testaments and as being used by Christians alone. However, that is only part of the truth. Jews refer to the first part of the Christian Bible as their Bible and that makes the Bible unique. It is the only holy book which is shared between two different religions.

The Jewish scriptures

The Bible as we know today is made up of the sacred scriptures of two religions – Christianity and its much older parent, Judaism. Jewish people have as their Bible what Christians call the Old Testament. Jews, however, do not refer to their scriptures by this name, since it suggests something that is out-of-date or replaced by something more recent. Nor do Jewish people use the New Testament. Whilst the Jewish and Christian faiths may have the same roots, they have since become very different.

What Christians call the Old Testament is known in Judaism as **Tenak**. This is made up of the following.

- The Torah or Law (**T**). This is the most important part of the Jewish scriptures and refers to the first five books of the Bible.

This man is reading from a scroll containing the most important part of the Jewish Scriptures. What is this part called?

- The Nebi'im or Prophets (**N**). The prophets were men and women who spoke with the authority of God.

- The Ketub'im or Writings (**K**). The remainder of the Jewish Scriptures.

We must remember that Jesus and his disciples were Jewish. The New Testament did not yet exist. They used the Torah, Nebi'im and Ketub'im as their scriptures. The Jewish scriptures were their guide. After the death of Jesus, his disciples shocked their Jewish friends when they insisted that parts of the Old Testament referred to Jesus. However, by the time this happened, Christians were not all Jews anyway and the Old Testament became less important in the Christian Church than the writings of Paul and others.

The Christian scriptures

The Bible as a whole, including both Old and New Testaments, is important for one faith only – Christianity. No other faith regards the whole Bible as sacred (holy), although, as we have seen, the first part is sacred for all Jews.

As we all know, there are other important religious faiths in the world which have millions of followers. What do these other religions think of the Bible and of the central figure in that book, Jesus of Nazareth?

Islam

In Islam, Jesus is a prophet. In fact, he is the last, and greatest, of a line of prophets stretching all the way back to Abraham. He is not, however, as important as Muhammad, the prophet of **Allah**. **Muslims** have great respect for Jesus, but the writing about him in the **Qur'an** is very different from that found in the New Testament.

Hinduism and Sikhism

In Hinduism and Sikhism there is also a great respect for Jesus. Neither of them, however, believe that he was God's Son, nor do they consider the Bible to be a sacred book alongside their own holy books.

What makes the Bible so special for all Christians is that it deals with both Jesus as a person *and* his teaching. These may be respected in other faiths, but to Christians they are sacred.

- Which scriptures did Jesus and his disciples know and use?
- What is the Christian attitude to the Old Testament?
- Why is the attitude of Christianity towards the Bible and Jesus Christ so different from that of other religions?

For your dictionary

Allah is the name used by Muslims to refer to God.
A **Muslim** is a person who has submitted to Allah.
The **Qur'an** is the holy book of Islam.
Tenak is the term used by Jews to describe their Bible, made up of the Torah (Law), Nebi'im (Prophets) and Ketub'im (Writings).

1 Three people are talking about the 'Bible':

A Jewish rabbi

The Bible started with the Jewish religion centuries before the Christians took it over. Our Bible belongs to us and can belong to no one else.

A university professor

The Bible is one of the greatest treasures of our civilisation. It really belongs to everyone – Jew and Christian – and not to one group in particular.

A Christian priest

For Christians the whole Bible is really concerned with Jesus of Nazareth and so it belongs to us.

In your own words, write a few sentences to say which of these opinions you have most sympathy with. (Could there be an element of truth in all three of them?)

2 Read the following two passages from the Bible:
- Psalm 22.
- Isaiah 53.

a How many similarities can you find between these two passages and the life of Jesus?
b What conclusion might you draw from these similarities?
c What does this tell us about how early Christians saw Jesus?

How was the Bible translated?

When the books of the Bible were first written, none of them were in English. The Old Testament was written in the Hebrew language and the New Testament in Greek. After many centuries the Bible was first translated into Latin and then, much later, into English.

Hebrew

You can see from the photograph below what a passage from the Old Testament in Hebrew looks like. Although, like English, Hebrew starts from the top of the page, it is, unlike English, written from right to left. This means that the first word on a page of Hebrew is found in the top, right-hand corner.

Anyone who tries to learn Hebrew will find that there is another problem. There are two ways of writing the language:

- In the first ('unpointed' Hebrew) only the consonants are included. This makes it very difficult to read.

- In the second, the vowels are included and these are written as dots and dashes above and below the consonants (called 'pointed' Hebrew). The vowels were placed above and below the line because the original text was so sacred it could not be marked.

This Hebrew text shows part of the first chapter of the Bible, Genesis. What is unusual about the way that Hebrew is written?

Greek

Reading Greek is much easier than Hebrew, since the vowels are always included. One complication is that, whilst the New Testament was originally written in Greek, this was not the language spoken by Jesus and his followers. That was **Aramaic** although hardly a trace of that language survives in the New Testament.

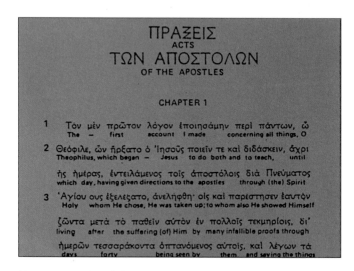

How many Greek letters can you see which look like their English equivalents?

Translations of the Bible

The first translation of the Bible into English was made by John Wycliffe and his followers (who were called Lollards) in the fourteenth century. They did not translate from the original Hebrew and Greek, but from a Latin version of the Bible made in the fourth century. This was called the **Vulgate**.

The first complete English version of the Bible to be printed was made by Miles Coverdale in 1535. He was translating into the English of his time and that was very different from the English of today.

Most Christians still think that the most beautiful translation of the Bible was that published in 1611 on the instructions of King James I and known as the Authorised Version. If you have a copy of the Bible at home, it may well be of this version. The king brought together a team of 54 scholars to work on a translation which was intended to replace all other translations. It was not long before a copy of this translation was placed in every parish church in the country.

℃ The fyrst Chapter.

This is the first page (the opening of Genesis) from the Great Bible, printed in England in 1539. Try to write out a part of the text in modern English.

The Authorised Version is still used in some churches today. For more than 300 years the translation went unchallenged. In the last hundred years, however, many new translations have been published. They include:

- the Revised Version, 1881.
- the Revised Standard Version, 1952.
- the Jerusalem Bible, 1966.
- the Revised English Bible, 1989.

Even after all these years the Bible continues to sell more copies than any other book. Between 1800 and 1990, around 3,000,000,000 (three thousand million) copies of the Bible are thought to have been printed worldwide. Each year over 10,000,000 copies of the Bible are sold throughout the world.

For your dictionary

Aramaic was the language spoken in Palestine at the time of Jesus.

The **Vulgate** was a Latin version of the Bible prepared by St Jerome between the years 354 and 404.

- In which languages were the Old and New Testaments originally written?
- Which language did Jesus and his disciples use?
- Who first translated the Bible into English?

1 Here are two translations of the same verse – John 3.16. Read both of them carefully.

For God so loved the world, that he gave his only begotten Son, that whosoever believeth in him should not perish but have everlasting life.

(The Authorised Version, 1611)

God so loved the world that he gave his only Son, that everyone who has faith in him may not perish but have eternal life.

(The Revised English Bible, 1989)

What differences do you notice between the two translations? Which translation do you prefer? Why?

2 It is important to remember that the early translators of the Bible, like John Wycliffe, copied out each word by hand. To get some idea of how tiring (and time-consuming!) this must have been, try this simple test.

a Open a Bible at random.
b Work out just where the halfway point is on the page facing you.
c Time yourself as you copy out the top half of the page.
d Multiply the time by 2.
e Multiply the answer that you have by the number of pages in your Bible.
(Remember – this is just the time it would take to *copy* the Bible out. Wycliffe and his friends were also *translating* it as they went along!
P.S. How does your wrist feel?)

How is the Bible used?

If you stay in any hotel in Britain you are likely to find a Gideon Bible by your bedside. The Gideons is an international organisation of Christian businessmen dedicated to placing a copy of the Bible in as many places as possible. They believe that the Bible should not only be used in public worship but also in private prayer and devotion.

The Bible in private devotion

Most Christians feel that reading the Bible regularly at home helps them to understand more about God and his will for their lives. They usually try to follow a clear plan in their Bible reading. If they belong to a Roman Catholic or Anglican Church they may follow a **lectionary** which has a set Bible reading for each day of the year. Alternatively, they may use Bible-reading notes from such organisations as the Scripture Union or the International Bible Reading Fellowship. These notes not only follow a set pattern but also explain the passage that is being read.

Christians reading the Bible on their own usually do so slowly, to allow the meaning of the passage to become clear. In this way they are able to discover whether the passage can guide or help them in their daily lives. Often it can offer strength or guidance when they are unhappy or depressed. Sometimes it may help with an important decision that has to be made.

Christians often come together informally in small groups to study the Bible. This means that they are able to share what they learn with each other. In many Churches time is set aside, particularly during **Lent** (the weeks leading up to **Easter**) so that a serious study of the Bible can take place.

For your dictionary

Easter is the time of year when Christians celebrate the death and resurrection of Jesus.
A **lectionary** is a plan for reading the Bible in church or in private.
Lent is the time of reflection observed by many Christians in the period before Easter.
The **pulpit** is the raised platform in a church from which the sermon is preached.

What might this Christian hope to gain from reading the Bible?

The Bible in public worship

Most church services have two readings from the Bible. In Nonconformist services these passages are chosen by the person leading the service, but in Anglican and Roman Catholic services a set pattern is followed – as laid down in the lectionary. Usually one reading is taken from the Old Testament and one from the New Testament. In the service of Communion another reading, from one of the Epistles, is often included.

In Anglican, Catholic and Orthodox services, the Gospel reading is given greater importance than the other readings. This is indicated by:

- the Gospel being carried into the middle of the congregation and being surrounded by a cross-bearer and candle-holders.

- only allowing the Gospel to be read by a priest or a deacon. Before reading, the priest makes the sign of the cross over himself – with many in the congregation often doing the same. This symbolic gesture indicates that the words of scripture will be on their lips, in their heart and in their mind.

- the people remaining standing during the Gospel reading to demonstrate both their reverence for it and their willingness to act upon it.

In Nonconformist Churches, where a great emphasis is laid upon the preaching of the Bible, it is often carried into the **pulpit** before the service begins. In these churches, the pulpit, the focal-point of the church, is the place from which the message of the Bible is proclaimed.

- What do Christians often use to help them to understand a passage from the Bible?
- What is a lectionary?
- How do many Churches show their great respect for the Gospels?

1 Look at this picture carefully. Imagine that you have to choose one passage from the Gospels for this person to talk about.

a Which passage would you choose?
b Write a paragraph explaining why you have chosen this passage.
c Imagine that you are the preacher in the picture. What would you say about the passage you have chosen?

2 a Write down as many reasons as you can for the Gideons wanting to place a Bible in as many places as possible.

b It might be possible to arrange for a representative from the Gideons to visit your class. If so, try to find out:

- how the Gideons started.
- why they want to place the Bible wherever possible.
- whether people actually read the Gideon Bibles.
- where the money comes from for their work.

What authority does the Bible have?

Although Christians may use other books in their worship and personal devotion, none of them carries the same authority as the Bible. But what is it that makes the Bible so special? What is the authority that it has for many people? Where does that authority come from?

Where does the authority come from?

When a Christian is confused about some matter of belief or behaviour, where does he or she turn for advice or guidance? There are three alternatives:

- To the Bible, which some believe to be 'the Word of God'.

- To the Church.

- To their own conscience, or advice from others.

If a Christian needs an answer to a particular problem they may turn to one, two or even all three of these. For most Protestants the authority of the Bible is greater than that of the Church. Roman Catholics, however, believe that the Bible can only be interpreted by the Church, so they stress the authority of the Church over that of the Bible. The Orthodox Church tends to agree with the Catholic point of view.

Different attitudes towards the Bible

Do all Christians believe everything that they read in the Bible? The Bible is, for all Christians, in some sense the Word of God. As they read it, they hope to hear the spirit of God speaking to them. Yet there are different ways of understanding just what this means:

1   Some people think that the Bible was dictated directly by God to the writers, as if they were taking down notes. If this is the case, then everything in the Bible must be true. The Bible really is therefore the Word of God – word for word.

2   Some Christians believe that the personalities of the writers of the Biblical books are an important part of what they wrote. The Bible is therefore not *directly* the Word of God. The Bible contains great ideas and thoughts which do come directly from God, that God spoke through the Old Testament prophets, and that God was in Jesus. Yet some parts of the Bible are obviously more important than others, and Christians must bear this in mind when they are reading it.

3   Other Christians believe that there are insights about God and human nature in the Bible, as there are in other writers like Shakespeare or Jane Austen. The Bible writers may indeed have deep understanding which can help others to know about God, but they still made many mistakes. For instance, many of their ideas are expressed in a way that might have made sense in the ancient world, but do not mean very much to us today – that God created the world in six days; that the earth is flat; that the heavens fit over the earth like a dome. We now have alternative explanations. We must always look for the meaning behind the words of the Bible.

Bear in mind these different viewpoints as you find out more about the Bible, and try to make up your mind which you agree with.

The Queen is shown receiving a copy of the Bible at her Coronation in 1953. Can you find out why this happens at the coronation of each British monarch?

The Bible in the modern world

There are two important questions to consider:

1   How can a book that was written so long ago, and in a world so different to ours, have anything to say to us today?

2   Does the Bible have anything to say today and, if so, what is it?

There are many important issues in the modern world which were unknown when the Bible was written – unemployment, pollution and test-tube babies, for example. Many Christians would still insist that the basic teaching and message of the Bible do not change over time, but others would argue that the Bible was written for a very different age and needs to be re-interpreted in the light of modern events. Whatever we make of the Bible, we cannot simply accept it just as it stands.

- What do we mean when we refer to the Bible as 'the Word of God'?
- What are the different attitudes of Protestants and Roman Catholics towards the authority of the Bible and of the Church?
- What do most Christians believe about the Bible?

1 Here are three very different attitudes towards the Bible.

Try to explain in your own words the differences between these three attitudes to the Bible.

2 Decide, with the help of your teacher, the approach that people with each of the attitudes in Exercise 1 would take to the following three passages from the Bible.

Joshua and the falling down of the walls of Jericho (Joshua 6)

Jesus feeding 5,000 men, women and children (Mark 6.33–44)

St Paul and the role of women (Ephesians 5.21–24)

Index

Page references in bold indicate that the word is defined on this page in the 'For your dictionary' box.